Author's Acknowledgments

I give praise and thanks to Divine Spirit, for giving me the guidance, direction, and inspiration in writing this book. I give thanks for my Soulmate Lester for all his love and support day to day, and to the Universe that timed our incarnations such that he and I would connect in this lifetime and share in our life's work together. I also give thanks to family and friends for their support. Thanks to: Vicktorya Stone for her thoughtfulness and care in editing this work, Richard Haeger for graphics and cover design and France-Marie Haeger for the art work. Thanks to those who gave me feedback on the manuscript which include: Lisa Connelly, Joan Fox, Charlie Billikas, Donna Mitchell-Moniak, Monique Pommier, Donna Bivens, Donald Roach, and Rick Prater. Finally, thanks to Michael Robbins, for his demonstration of fiery will.

On The Way
To Finding
Your Soulmate

By
Terri Nelson

ON THE WAY
TO FINDING
YOUR SOULMATE

Terri Nelson

First Edition

Published by: ABOVE THE DIN PUBLISHING
P.O. Box 2506
Jamaica Plain, MA 02130

Copyright © 1996 by Terri Nelson
First Printing
Printed in the United States of America
Library of Congress Catalog card number 97-73855
Nelson, Terri
ISBN 0-9659600-3-X

Edited by Vicktorya Stone
Cover graphics by Richard Haeger
Cover art by France-Marie Haeger

Introduction

Is this the lifetime in which you will meet your Soulmate on this earthly plane? Do you have the strong desire and commitment to make this event manifest on earth?

This book is about a Spiritual Journey. A journey which includes finding your Soulmate. A Soulmate is that special someone unlike any other who touches your inner being and stirs your remembrance of your Divinity within. A Soulmate is someone who comes into your life as you follow a spiritual path. It is not someone you put your whole life energy into finding—forgetting about your spiritual mission. A Soulmate is someone we meet and re-meet along our path of return to God.

This book is for singles and couples who are seeking to know a harmonious relationship with their mate on earth. It awakens you to the depth of spiritual connection that you may seek and find in a Soulmate, or unveil in your current union. This book guides you through many steps, meditations, prayers and exercises. These reveal that your search to find your Soulmate is an inner one and not an outer one. You are aided to do the inner work to raise your vibration so that you will naturally attract one another on a spiritual level. Opening to the Universe, finding that Sacred space within, working on self

esteem and self forgiveness, are just some of the many steps you are guided through. These steps help remove the things that act as blockages in your receipt of the gift of a harmonious and loving union.

Your attunement with your own Soul will open you to the abundance and prosperity that the Universe has in store for you. Just one of the many blessings of this attunement will be the increased awareness and connection with the Soul of the mate who is divinely and perfectly suited for you. It reveals how to attune to the energy of your Soulmate mate even while he or she still remains invisible to your physical eyes so that recognition can occur when the time comes for you to actually meet on the physical plane.

This book is for those who seek to live and experience wholeness, seek to bring their wholeness to a union with a mate, and seek to work together interdependently. It is for those who desire to promote the highest and greatest good in themselves and their mates and to help one another to unfold spiritually even if it means—letting one another go.

This book is not for those who are seeking a mate to glorify them but for those who are seeking to glorify God and may happen to find a Soulmate along the way. This book is not for those who are addicted to the love of being loved as an end point in itself. The quality of love is like a magnet. There is magnetic attraction in love. This book is for you if you are willing to use the magnetic and attractive *power of love to draw yourself and your mate toward the Light and together also draw others in your midst toward this same Light. Those who are addicted to love, sex and romance should first deal with issues of co-dependency and establishing spiritual connectedness in their lives in order to be prepared for a Soulmate union.*

Not every lifetime includes this type of quest. This book offers special instruction to those who strongly desire Soulmate union and feel their inner wisdom is guiding them to seek such unions. This book is for those on a spiritual path who are seeking full realization of their Divinity which includes a spirit-filled union with a mate that reflects this Divinity.

About the Author

From the time I first opened my conscious eyes I have known a deep communion with God.

Terri Nelson, L.I.C.S.W., M.S.W., M.S.E.P, Reiki Master, is a Holistic Psychotherapist. Her training has included both traditional and esoteric approaches to healing. She has a Bachelor of Science in Psychology, a Masters in Social Work, a Masters in the Science of Esoteric Psychology and is a Ph.D.E. candidate in Esoteric Studies.

The author has a private practice which uses a variety of healing methods. She is also a clinician in a major Health Maintenance Organization providing psychotherapy in adult mental health. She is a teacher and a student of the Ageless Wisdom and has a particular interest in understanding and balancing energy in relationships. She gives lectures and seminars on a variety of psychospiritual subjects.

Table of Contents

Chapter One

On The Way To Finding Your Soulmate

In April 1994, I was on a retreat, deep in meditation. This was a silent retreat in which I would not speak to or be spoken to by the outside world for a few days. It was in this silence that Spirit revealed to me that I would write this book. The message was quite clear. This guidance spoke the words, "You have already conceived this book. You merely need to go to your journals, take excerpts of what is written there and add commentary to provide clarity."

Well, I thought, I had been keeping a journal of my experiences *On The Way To Finding My Soulmate*. My Soulmate Lester and I met on December 24, 1985, and we have been sharing a beautifully Soulful union ever since. So, to the still small voice that had just spoken to me, I inwardly spoke the words, "Yes, of course I will write this book. After all, it is time."

Spirit is what guides me to live, love and work more in accord with the will of God and the divine plan for my life. At times I may feel more or less in alignment with Spirit depending on how attuned, rested, and alert I am. Yet, this inner wisdom and guidance is there for me and it is there for you. I have always tried to listen to this inner wisdom and guidance.

From about the age of three or four, when I first remember opening my conscious eyes, I have had a deep communion with Spirit, Father, Mother, God, Goddess. I recall how at that age I would sometimes play in front of the bathroom mirror. If I balanced myself just right by standing on the bathtub while holding onto the bathroom sink I would be tall enough to catch my reflection in a corner of the mirror. Perched there, I would spend time gazing into my eyes. I knew even at this early age that there was *a presence behind my eyes.* I was convinced that if I looked long enough and hard enough that I would be able to see it. Somehow, I knew this presence was in me but was much bigger than me. I learned to see and sense this presence in others and to later be guided by what I now know to be the Divine presence of God or Spirit.

So, as with all things on my life's journey, I listened for inner guidance from Spirit on the way to finding my Soulmate. It was this guidance that led me through the steps of actually manifesting this event on the earthly or physical plane. This quest and longing for this other, my Soulmate, was deep in my subconscious from the time I was born. Finding and knowing real love has always been important to me. That you have chosen to read this book is an indication that answering questions about true love and union with your Soulmate is also important to you at this point in your journey.

In what follows I will share my experiences and the things that Spirit revealed to me leading up to the union with my Soulmate. On the way to finding my Soulmate, I moved from a place of only being able to experience him in my mind's eye to a place of being able to actually meet and behold him in his earthly/physical plane manifestation.

I have been guided by Spirit through a series of steps in making what was *invisible* to me to *finally visible.* The gulf from one to the other needs to be spanned in order to connect with your Soulmate. This book is about what that gulf felt like for me and the work I needed to do to span it. It is offered as a guide to you *On The Way To Finding Your Soulmate.*

I will share reflections from my life experiences which shaped who I am in this lifetime. I do not feel like I am a beginner in my quest for a Soulmate relationship. I began my search many lifetimes ago. As such, I will include reflections of my experiences as a Soul who has been journeying through many incarnations extracting the essence of life's lessons.

I also share my clinical experiences as a holistic psychotherapist who has been working in the mental health field since 1980. My approach has been to try to help others attune to their own inner wisdom so that it may guide them in their own healing. In facilitating this healing process I support others to become aware of what is going on within them spiritually, mentally, emotionally, and physically. I ask clients, What do you need to do to heal yourself, feel joy, and experience life fulfillment?

I am profoundly touched by the human experience and particularly by the work I do with couples in therapy as they strive to have Spirit and Soul filled unions together as mates. As an African American woman, I have worked extensively with the African American community and the perspective shared in this book is certainly influenced by but not limited to this orientation.

Throughout the book I outline steps, meditations, prayers, exercises and affirmations which support your spiritual alignment in manifesting the event of Soulmate union. Each time that the following words appear, take a moment to close your eyes and take a few deep breaths.

- ◆ **STEP**
- ◆ **MEDITATION**
- ◆ **PRAYER**
- ◆ **EXERCISE**
- ◆ **AFFIRMATION**

As you breathe in, experience a sense of peace, calm and relaxation. As you breathe out clear the space within and around you of any interference. Take some time to hold in mind each of the thoughts that will follow these words.

Additionally, this book will include excerpts from my journals which will appear in italicized and bold print, as in the following:

__August 17, 1983__

__Dear God, Father of My Soul,__
__I said that I would not become lost in fantasy or my imaginings. What would it accomplish anyway? Yet my mind contin- ues to wonder to thoughts of my Soulmate. So much so that I cannot think or do much else. The thoughts are pleasant. It is a dream picture, in which he and I meet and thoroughly connect.__

__It is a vision in which everything turns out all right.__

STEP 1

Being Clear On What You Want
And Do Not Want

Finding a Soulmate is not a far off event that should forever remain in the realm of fantasy or imaginings. It is an event that can become substantive, touching down in your life, anchored in your reality. It requires that you are clear on what you want and what you do not want.

There were many years of my being unhappy in my first marriage and I had begun to mourn the loss of the relationship long before we parted physically. However, during those years, deep within my heart there was a yearning for my Soulmate that was always beckoning me to the future that is revealed in this book.

I knew for years before separating from my first husband that I did not want to leave that relationship to find just any mate. I wanted to find my Soulmate. Furthermore, I did not want finding my Soulmate to be one of trial and error, hit or miss, going from one dating situation to the next.

I wanted finding my Soulmate to be a process of precision, intelligently and divinely guided. I did not want to make finding my Soulmate my life's work. Instead, I wanted to meet my Soulmate as soon as possible so that we could share in our life work together, helping and supporting one another.

STEP 2

Opening To Guidance
From Spirit

I want to communicate to you that I have been guided by Spirit in my quest to find my Soulmate and that you may also be guided in your quest to find your Soulmate! I attuned to Spirit and Spirit led me.

Foremost, Spirit gave me the vision and the strong desire for Soulmate union. Even though I knew such unions existed I grumbled at times about having this vision and strong desire. Both continually spurred me in a quest for something I could not see and after something I did not know I could attain. All I knew was that the desire and the vision would not go away.

I did not make a conscious decision to follow any particular steps or plan in invoking or asking the Universe for my Soulmate. I really did not know what steps I was taking or what I was doing. However, as I look back now I clearly see that Spirit led me to take the many steps described in this book. These steps aided my development so that the event of finding my Soulmate could be made manifest. I have now been guided to share these steps with you, in hope that they will aid you also. I am concerned about the condition of all human relationships on the planet. I am particularly concerned about the quality of relationships between men and women.

In finding my Soulmate I feel that I have been able to at least glimpse the depth of love, sharing and caring that can exist between mates. This relationship reveals to me that *we may truly know heaven on earth in our relationship with our mates.*

This book is about my journey to my Soulmate. My Soulmate Lester and I feel very blessed to be sharing a life together and we are filled with joy. We journey together embracing our human selves as we unfold into fuller realization of our God Selves. We face our trials and errors as humans striving towards this greater dawning of who we really are.

Naturally our Soulmate relationship does not reflect the heaven on earth, of which this book speaks, every minute of every day. Our relationship, like other relationships, requires energy and commitment to make it work, to keep the love flowing and to keep us evolving and growing as a couple. However, our relationship convinces me that there are tremendous rewards in holding the vision of creating heaven on earth in our union.

This book is about doing the inner work on yourself in order to more fully realize what a Soulmate relationship is and can embody and to then actualize this reality. We must hold the vision of harmony, peace, and optimal spiritual growth in our marriages. These unions should not be tombs of psychic assault, violence, spiritual and physical death, but sanctuaries and safe havens of maximal unfoldment for both mates and subsequently their children. This book is an encouragement to strive towards one another consciously in this vision long before you meet as mates.

On this planet, we have been so immersed in the painful experiences that recur in male and female relationships. For this reason some of what you read in this book may seem too idealistic, too out of reach or too farfetched. But reaching for higher realms in which to reside with our mates and holding steadfast to our ideal of harmonious and Soul-filled unions is what we must do. In this way we contribute to the spiritualization of the earth by bringing a measure of heaven into how we live day to day with our mates.

STEP 3

Keeping A Journal

Keeping a journal was and still is a very important tool in my own healing and self discovery. A journal is a place to record your innermost thoughts, feelings, desires, aspirations, failures, fantasies, dreams, and more. It is a place to record life situations and events and how you respond to them. Over time you are able to see your changing thoughts and moods and to observe your patterns.

By observing your patterns you increase your awareness of your enduring responses to life events. From this awareness flows valuable insights into how you may change your patterns so that your actions may increasingly yield a set of consequences that you feel better and better about.

Your journal can guide you to see more clearly how to navigate through obstacles in your life. This allows you to make certain adjustments in order to minimize the effects of changing circumstances. Your journal points out your strengths and weaknesses. It helps point out the more vulnerable times of the week, month or year, thus allowing you to take certain steps or precautions to take care of your needs, such as getting more rest.

My journal has always been there for me. It has been there during times in my first marriage when I would awake in the middle of the night, feel lonely and would wish I had someone to talk to. I would begin my journal entries by addressing them to the Higher or Master Consciousness or Spirit within me. Thus, I would write, Dear God, Father, Mother of My Soul.

August 21, 1983

Dear God, Father, Mother of My Soul,
I could settle for life as it is. I could
accept the pleasures of the senses that it
brings. But I cannot.
If all I do in my lifetime is move away
from the things that assault me spiritu-
ally then I would have done something. I
may never have what I want but if this be
so then I choose not to accept the things I
do not want. Instead, I choose to spend my
life in search of something better. I want
to search for something better.

I became convinced that there must be a process whereby events that we truly desire can be made manifest in our lifetime. This book is about that process.

NOTES

Chapter Two

What Is A Soulmate? The Spiritual Connection And Soulmates

What does it mean to begin a quest for a Soulmate union? I believe that: *A Soulmate is that one who is divinely and perfectly suited for you spiritually, mentally, emotionally and physically. He or she is that being who takes away the loneliness and longing completely, fosters a deep and abiding sense of fulfillment in you and enhances the expression of your life purpose. A Soulmate is that special someone unlike any other who touches your inner being and stirs your remembrance of your Divinity within.*

As mentioned, this quest and longing for this other, my Soulmate, was deep in my subconscious from the time I was born. It is in your subconscious also, just waiting to be awakened, if it has not already. Finding and knowing real love has always been important to me. I knew that having a relationship on earth with a mate that reflected God's love for me was my divine inheritance. I wanted to be in a relationship through which I could more directly experience God's love and presence in my life.

My first husband Jay (not his real name) and I connected emotionally and physically. I met him when I was seventeen and we were together seventeen years. He was a loving and good person. I could not have remained with him all those years if this were not so. Yet we did not connect mentally and spiritually. He did not talk to me very much and when we did talk there were limits to what we could share together and where we could go in our conversation. We did not share similar interests. Though we lived together we lived in separate worlds. Over the years of our marriage we grew further and further apart, *even connecting less and less emotionally and physically.* I felt tremendous loneliness in my relationship with Jay. *Where was I to go with the other parts of myself?* I felt mentally hungry and spiritually starved in the relationship.

The spiritual, mental, emotional, and physical dimensions of ourselves represent points of contact, connection, and communication that we can have with our mate. When we resonate with a mate on these levels we experience more of an ease in being together. There is more sharing and receptivity to one another's views, feelings, and life direction. Out of this resonance comes an ease at cohabiting and building a life together. There is a natural tendency to recognize the life purpose of each other and the life purpose of the union you share together as mates. Both of you work to support the active unfolding of that purpose in each other and in the union.

In response to the loneliness I felt in my first marriage, I turned to other people to meet my mental and spiritual needs, sharing my gifts of mind and spirit with them in return. Nevertheless, meeting my needs in this way led me to feel quite compartmentalized in my relationship with Jay. Earlier in our relationship I would ask him, "Why do you think you are here on earth, what have you come to do? He would respond, "I don't think about that stuff." His response each time both amazed and saddened me.

I would ponder the meaning of life often. I could not imagine not being curious about these things. I wanted him to touch me deeply—to touch my Soul. I wanted to touch his Soul. I wanted us to live and share in a world of depth and meaning. Yet with Jay I could not find his depth.

Equally disheartening was the fact that I could not see my own depth in him, echoed and reflected back to me. We had reached a plateau and could not mutually scale a deeper depth nor ascend to a greater level of aliveness, spiritual connection and commitment in our relatedness. Additionally there seemed to be an impenetrable wall between us. He did not seem to be trying to connect with his own essence—the Soul and source of his being. Therefore, he was not available to connect with mine.

This lack of conscious, enlivened, connection between the spiritual life essence in me and the spiritual life essence in him was excruciatingly painful for me. It meant so much to me to be able make a spiritual connection with my mate. He was the one being on the planet with whom I spent so much of my life.

In time, a dullness and dimming set in the relationship. I questioned him less and less about touching life's mysteries more deeply with me. Ultimately, touching one another more deeply became more and more remote. I stopped asking him to share his depth with me or to go to my depths to find out where I lived. By then, I was convinced that whatever his sense of spiritual connection had been, I had just plain failed to tap into it.

In times of sadness and loneliness, I would secretly think about another. During the day I would think about him, my Soulmate. I would also meet my Soulmate in my dreams at night. In my daily and nightly thoughts of him the energy of my Soulmate was always very loving, attentive, and sensitive to my needs. Sometimes my Soulmate assumed the face of one man, sometimes the face of another. However, it was more about a *quality of energy* and how he made me feel rather than who he was or what he looked like.

STEP 4

Sensing Your Soulmate

Begin by imagining what he or she feels like to you. Next try to experience what he or she looks like. Do not be discouraged if you only have a vague outline that begins to fill in more over time. As we will see later, it is his or her energy that you are trying to attune to.

What qualities does your Soulmate radiate as you visualize him or her? For example, does he or she feel warm, strong, outgoing, or sensitive to you? How does this energy move? What shape or form does it take? What else do you begin to experience?

I always felt comforted during the moments I spent thinking about my Soulmate. In the morning, after dreaming about him, I awoke with a sense of peace and ease, feeling very centered deep within myself. During the day my thoughts of him brought me renewed strength and zest for life and living. Tapping into this energy is something that is available to you.

MEDITATION

Sensing Your Soulmate

Sitting right where you are in this moment
imagine warm and loving energy
being radiated to you by your Soulmate.

Begin to sense his or her presence.
Try to visualize him or her.

Imagine sharing your life with a mate
within this loving radiance of energy.

There is a spiritual connection that you experience in Soulmate unions. With Soulmates there is the ability to see your whole self in the other. Like your reflection in a full length mirror, your Soulmate is the one who is able to capture your *whole image*. You feel fully contained and reflected in the other. This allows you to share your *whole self*. You do not leave parts of yourself out and you can give your whole self freely.

In a Soulmate union each partner is fully contained and reflected in the other and it is *an exquisitely wonderful feeling*. Have you ever noticed how some mirrors truncate parts of your head, or arms, or legs? Similarly, some relationships truncate parts of who you are spiritually, mentally, emotionally or physically. This leads to a sense of compartmentalization.

Your Soulmate can come to know you better than any other being on the planet. Has anyone ever told you that he or she *loves you*, yet you experience deep in your heart that he or she does not even *know you*? What is it to be loved by another if he or she does not know you?

STEP 5

Knowing Yourself

Of course knowing yourself is of paramount importance. I had to get to know and love myself more fully on the way to finding my Soulmate so that I could know and love him more fully when the time came for us to finally meet.

The ancient injunction to 'Know Thy Self' directs us toward self knowledge and discovery. Life experience and time helps us in getting to know who we are. At the beginning of my first marriage, I did not have much experience in sorting out who I was before I found myself in a committed relationship with another. I needed to understand more my world view, my emotions, and my own spiritual awareness and connection with God.

In knowing who you are you are clearer on what you want in a relationship with your Soulmate. You will be clearer on what qualities you bring to the relationship in terms of your strengths and your weaknesses.

In experiencing this union of Soulmates there is the awareness that no one else has ever *recognized you* in this way before—that is, unless you have had other Soulmate encounters in this lifetime. There is also the awareness that if no one else ever again recognized, re-flected, and contained you in this lifetime, the sheer memory of this sacred encounter and the validation it brings of your full being will last you for a lifetime—if not lifetimes. For example, when we are away from home and longing to be there, we can be comforted and filled with a sense of warmth, love and security through our thoughts and good memories of what being *home* feels like. Similarly, remembering the depth of connection that has been experienced in a Soulmate union gives an en-during and comforting sense of well being.

When Soulmates meet there is a magnetic attraction to one another and an electrifying recognition of each other. There is a sense that you have known this person before and experienced one another's energy before.

MEDITATION

**Soulmate Union
And Your Union With God**

As the Soul journeys through many lifetimes
or incarnations, imagine a time when
your Soul encountered another Soul,
and together you both struck a high note of
spiritual vibration that was most reminiscent
of your divine unity with God.

In his book, <u>Finding Your Soulmate</u>, Russ Michaels states that, "Memories from the ancient past return to hold their enticing image before us. Somewhere in the distant night of time, one special someone meant more to our soul than any other. This wondrous remembrance lifts our hearts and turns our minds' gaze toward this one brilliant star rising in the future heavens."

According to Michaels, "A Soulmate means someone ... who is so perfectly matched and intertwined with our own unique destiny, that we experience a flood of exquisite bliss whenever the circumstances of life bring us together ... Our true mate is the one who is like ourselves spiritually." [1]

There are different ways to understand the concept of a Soulmate. If a Soulmate is one who is like ourselves spiritually then we may even consider that we have more than one or even many Soulmates. For example, a Soulmate may be a best friend, a teacher, a co-worker, or relative. Some Soulmate unions may be romantic and sexual, some may not. As a heterosexual woman I was seeking union with a heterosexual man, a union that would be spiritual, romantic and sexual. I desired to share my life with him fully and totally. What I call a *True Soulmate* is *union with that one whom you are perfectly and divinely suited for on all planes, spiritual, mental, emotional and physical.*

Michaels says that, "They are on the same soul ray during manifestation." He further writes, "It seemed very clear to us that we had walked hand in hand many times in many lives before ... an eternal love out of a misty past that had only to be remembered to be renewed." [2]

There is a similarity in vibration that you experience with your Soulmate and recognize instantly because his or her touch is so familiar to you. I experience a strong and compelling spiritual connection with my Soulmate Lester. I know we have loved one another in other lifetimes. He is so familiar to me. At times when we embrace we just experience the harmony of our vibration together. Like a baby remembering its mother's heart-beat there is the recognition of our Souls' vibration and our Souls' intent.

So often we hear the expression, Where is your other half? This is not the case in Soulmate unions. In Soulmate unions there is a sharing in each other's *wholeness* versus each one making the other whole. It is in knowing yourself that you experience your wholeness. As we strive to know and experience our own wholeness we become more aware of the wholeness in our mate. This wholeness fosters an interdependence which in turn fosters an integrative and expanding sense of wholeness in both mates.

MEDITATION

Bringing Out The Best In You

Soulmate unions bring out
the best in both of you.
Have you been in a relationship that
you felt brought out the worst in you?

Imagine a union that unfolds
and reveals the best in you.

What would you both be doing together?
What would you both share together?

STEP 6

Embracing Your Divinity—
Soulmate Unions And Your
Spiritual Union With God

Soulmates strengthen your unity and connection with God and allow a glimpse, if not a sustained experience, of that Divine unity. In other words, a union of Soulmates is one of the closest relationships on earth to experiencing God's love. We feel the love of God being expressed through the instrument of this other being. The love of God coming through our Soulmate makes God's love for us tangible on earth. When there is an absence of love in male and female relationships, there can be a blotting out of the Soul light of each partner. Both can feel more disconnected from their divinity as they continue in a relationship that denies their goodness and affirms a negative image of who they are.

In a Soulmate union you can experience God's love on earth more fully. You feel the presence of God's love in and through your Soulmate. *You can see God behind the eyes of your mate.* Even though that mate makes human errors, the Light and Love of God always radiates out to you. Love is reflected in Love.

Come to accept and experience your divinity, your Godliness within. Anticipate and expect that your relationship with your Soulmate will reflect that divinity. In my life with Lester I feel the tangible presence and expression of God's love for me coming through him. His loving radiance affirms my divinity within and God's divine love for me. Elizbeth Haitch in <u>The Initiation</u> writes: "... O' my sweet beloved! I've been looking for you for a long, long time, for an eternity, ever since we fell out of the Garden of Eden and became separated from each other. At last I've found you! ... You belong to me and I belong to you. We supplement each other completely. Do you feel the irresistible power of attraction that links us ... draws us closer ... together? ... We are the living reflected images of each other, and we belong together. You carry me about in your subconscious, just as I carry you in mine, and even without wanting to we seek each other with the irresistible attractive force that comes from our belonging together in the paradisiacal state." [3]

In Soulmate unions we have a wonderful opportunity to strengthen our connection with God and to see our divinity reflected in our mate. The journey is from God to God. A Soulmate is someone on our path who aids us in this journey and reflects our progress.

MEDITATION

God's Love Radiating To You
Through Your Soulmate

Close your eyes and imagine your Soulmate.

Now imagine God's love for you coming
through him or her making God's presence
and love for you tangible on earth.
Experience this loving presence now.

Later, when you are outside of meditation,
try to remember this feeling as you are
going about your daily activities.

STEP 7

Attuning To
Your Life Purpose

Soulmate unions bring clarity, enhanced expression, and fulfillment to your own Soul purpose. I have always asked Spirit, God, Goddess, Why am I here? Why have I incarnated or come into being? What have I come to do on earth? These have always been burning questions for me. The answers to these questions have evolved over time and I remain ever open to the changing and evolving drama of my life purpose.

Do you know your life purpose? Your Soulmate plays a part in your Divine reason, meaning, and purpose for being. Prior to, or even at the same time you begin invoking the Universe for your Soulmate, it is important for you to seek understanding of your life purpose.

MEDITATION

Life Purpose

Ask yourself,
Why have I incarnated?

What have I come to do?

What is it that I can do easily,
effortlessly, joyously and tirelessly?

The answer to these questions brings you closer to knowing and fulfilling your life purpose. Open to the response. With the desire to live purposefully comes the desire to love purposefully. It just seems to flow naturally out of this state of consciousness.

MEDITATION

Loving Purposefully

Imagine loving another purposefully!

Ask yourself, What is it that I want
from this loving relationship?

Again, open to
and await the response.

Soulmates share in and help each other to achieve their Soul purposes. Finding someone who supported me and whom I could support to be of greater service in the world is important to me.

At times we remark about the greatness achieved by a man or a woman in their lifetime. Often we are equally moved to take note of the greatness in the mate who has stood beside him or her.

There is an even deeper spiritual meaning to these words. Through union with your Soulmate you are aided to more completely fulfill your divine purpose on earth.

MEDITATION

Fulfilling Your Life Purpose
With Your Soulmate

Imagine working to fulfill your life purpose
with someone who is working in
harmony and accord with you.

What do you see yourself doing
as you creatively express who you are?

See your Soulmate supporting you to do the
work on earth that you have come to do.

I see my home as my nucleus. It is my place of power
and strength from which I radiate outward into the wider
world of service. Within the loving radiance of my
Soulmate, my energy moves with ease from this center
outward. In my first marriage, a non-Soulmate union,
my home at times felt like a vortex, draining and siphon-
ing off energy and hampering my efforts to even maintain family, let alone my efforts towards larger service.

In an expression of goodwill, Soulmates work to promote the spiritual growth of each other and aid the unfoldment and expression of the life purpose that each
has come to fulfill.

STEP 8

Keeping Your Focus
On The Light—
Keeping God First In Your Life

A Soulmate is someone on your path of return as you make your way toward God. Even though a Soulmate relationship fulfills many needs, only Divine Love can meet our every need.

Therefore, as Soulmates come to share their journeys together both should keep their focus on the Light of God. By maintaining this focus as a couple, this Light is kept ablaze in your consciousness. This Light becomes a guide that your union moves towards as you journey together. As you attune to God and his divine will for your union, you will more naturally attune to one another.

Maintaining this focus serves to shape and unfold your highest vision of your work in the world together. When couples turn away from their Higher Consciousness or God Self and focus too exclusively on each other or on something outside of the union, then discord, lack of direction, and a dwindling of the Light in the relationship can result. This is especially true when the focus has been too much on the personality or physical (form) aspect of each partner instead of on the indwelling, unifying Soul and guiding Spirit.

STEP 9

Considering Your Service
On Earth Together

My Soulmate Lester and I encourage and support each other's service on earth. We both strongly aspire to play and fulfill that part in the Divine Plan to bring heaven to earth that we have been blessed to glimpse and to understand. We both want to be in a loving union that supports our life purposes and Souls unfoldment versus a relationship that robs our energy, distracts, or even aborts our mission.

As we keep our focus on this guiding Light our foot-steps are naturally coordinated. We pray our earnest prayers that this guiding Light will lead us to continue our work together on sweet Mother Earth for as long as we both shall live. But *God is first* in both of our lives. We hope to remain together in this lifetime but we are committed to this Light, even if it takes us in different directions and we must part.

We affirm, "Thy Will Be Done." *The journey is from God to God. A Soulmate is someone we meet and re-meet along the path of return to God.*

NOTES

Chapter Three

The Aquarian Age
And The Increased Desire
For Soulmate Union

The Aquarian Age will bring about a spirit of Universal love, group consciousness, and cooperation. This energy will be felt on the level of romantic unions and the desire for union with one's Soulmate will intensify. As we grow to stand more in our own Soul awareness, the attractive power between Souls and the desire for union with our Soulmate will grow.

STEP 10

Standing More
In Soul Awareness

Living in Soul awareness is a higher organization of consciousness than living in the personality. The personality is composed of the physical/etheric, emotional/astral and mental vehicles or bodies. The physical/etheric body is the form that we can see and also the energy that vitalizes the form and keeps it healthy. The emotional/astral body is our feeling nature and desires. The mental body is the mind, and how we think, plan and reason. The personality is how we get our act together and keep it together. This is the energy that coordinates the physical, emotional and mental bodies so that these work in a purposeful way.

The Soul is your Higher purpose, meaning and reason for being. It is your conscious awareness and the accumulated wisdom of many lifetimes of experience. The Soul is the Light within, and your highest aspiration. It is the Higher Self which seeks more and more to imbue our daily life with wisdom, intelligent living, and selfless love. It is universal and unconditional love.

The Soul guides you to perform a service in the world that is larger than your limited personal sphere of existence and is in accord with the Divine will and purpose for your life. The Soul does its work through the personality by registering its intent on the personality. The personality is a vehicle or instrument for the Soul to manifest itself through on earth.

In this age comes the opportunity to transcend more the personality and to *stand more in Soul.* We might say at this level of awareness that we are Souls that have a personality rather than personalities that have a Soul.

MEDITATION

Soul Awareness

Reflect for a moment on all the challenges
that life presents to you as a personality.
Consider the personality bashing that goes on
in the world today, particularly in the media.
These kinds of assaults can erode your sense
of self and who you think you are.

Standing or living just in the personality
rather than in Soul limits your sense of Self.
If one lives or is most consciously focused in
the personality this contributes to why one
may feel so devastated when they come
under some personality attack.

In situations such as the loss of a job or the
breakup of a relationship, one may come to
feel all is lost and self identity is collapsed
into that one moment in time and space.
One identifies him or herself as the
instrument or personality rather than with
the indwelling Soul life that is directing the
form life of the personality instrument.

Standing in Soul Awareness allows you to
transcend beyond the more limited sense of
the *self* or personality and to know the *Self*
as limitless, boundless, and infinite.

AFFIRMATION

**Dis-identification
With The World Of Form**

I have this body, but I am not this body,
I am much, much more.

I have feelings, but I am not my feeling,
I am much, much, more.

I have thoughts, but I am not my thoughts,
I am much, much, more.

I am the Soul, I am Spirit

By standing in Soul awareness we can see more our Universal connection with all creation, our oneness with all things, our immortality. Who we are is not reducible or obliterated by any event in time and space.

It is no small wonder that people are looking for their Soulmate. We can see all around us, particularly in the field of physics, that the veil is lifting between science and spirituality, the form and the formless, matter and energy. There is an intensified quest to experience particular *qualities and essence* in our mates and less emphasis on just the form aspect or physical appearance.

Increasingly in our society, we are getting beneath the physical form and moving to more subtle levels of awareness in understanding the human makeup, and the makeup of the world around us.

It is here that we experience the energy vibration of our mates and the essence of their qualities. We are no longer captured by the shallowness of physical appearance. *When another speaks to us, we want him or her to speak the words that touch our Souls.* Knowing the energy makeup or vibration of a potential mate will be significant in finding your Soulmate.

Understanding the astrological and rayological [4] influences of your mate can also aid you in balancing and blending these energies. This will be part of the work of New Age Psychology. We are working toward the spiritualization of the planet as we work to infuse spiritual awareness in every aspect of human endeavor.

Our relationship with our mates is a very significant part of the spiritual transformation of our planet. We will shift our focus from just the matter or form aspect of physical existence as our spiritual awareness increases. We can see this happening all around us.

STEP 11

Seeing Below The Surface

Do you want to get beneath the surface with your mate and really know and experience who he or she is? Then you must be able to see below the surface and you will want to start by seeing yourself. Have you felt that things are becoming more and more confounded and that you cannot tell what is good for you through appearance only?

Appearances fool us. We are learning to see more, not by looking with our physical eyes, but by using our intuition as a way of knowing what and who is good for us. The use of the intuition in conjunction with a realistic understanding of the qualities we seek can guide us in looking below the surface in finding a mate.

We are now losing confidence in the external appearance of people and events. For example, choosing a day care provider to care for our child stirs us to search for the inner qualities of that caregiver at a deeper level. We cannot feel safe with someone just because they wear a certain kind of clothing, went to a particular school, live in a particular area, or is of particular race, religion, philosophy, and so on. We must rely on another kind of knowingness in choosing who or what is right for us.

As we evolve, children are being born with greater depth in seeing and knowing. They are able to see and read the energy field of people and situations around them and to detect higher and lower vibrations within these fields.

As we cultivate this more subtle seeing and knowing in ourselves, we can foster this development in our children. We can encourage them to speak about the things they see on more subtle energy levels rather than inhibit them. As children, we come with a natural inquisitiveness that the world around us does not always support. We live in a society that gives voice to racial, sexual, and economic oppressions. However, an oppression that is not often articulated is *Spiritual Oppression*. This can lead us to feel blocked in grasping and expressing an understanding of the underlying meaning of life.

The question becomes, how can we live more as a society that supports us to develop, explore, and express a conscious awareness of that which is invisible (unmanifest) and operating behind the visible (manifest) expression of life? I have wanted to understand the unmanifest operating behind the visible expression of life.

It is so important that you understand your relationship with your Soulmate while he or she is still in an unmanifest state or hidden from your view. You undertake this effort of awareness and focused attention on your Soulmate while he or she is unseen by you. You do this in order to make the event of union with your Soulmate manifest or come into your view.

On the way to finding your Soulmate you must seek to bring your awareness to what lay in back of what is visible. In this way you may sense and make contact with the energy of your Soulmate long before he or she ever appears.

STEP 12

Communicating With Your Soulmate: Wondering When He Or She May Appear— The Invisible Becomes Visible

Where is your Soulmate and when may he or she appear? I yearned so much for my Soulmate. *When I looked around and did not see him my heart cried out, Where is he to be found?* It is useful to ask yourself, How can what is invisible to me be made visible? When you look out and do not see your Soulmate anywhere, ask yourself, Is this being on the *inner* plane, not on the physical/earthly plane, or is this being on the physical or *outer* earthly plane? [5] Michaels says, "Our Soulmate may or may not be in physical incarnation at the same times as ourselves. In the latter case there is no possibility of meeting externally, even though we are bound together eternally at Soul levels." [6]

If this being is on earth, ask yourself, How may I locate him or her in time and space and communicate with him or her in the interim? What is the physical location of this being? Through my strong desire, how can my vision of union with my Soulmate be made to precipitate out on the physical plane so that I can reach out and touch him or her? In this latter case, I experienced this Soul to Soul realm of connection with my Soulmate. *Long before we connected on the physical plane I felt his warmth and touch even though he remained invisible to my physical eyes.* I desired union with my Soulmate so urgently I felt that surely he must be on the planet at this particular time. I felt surely he must be near. I was right! In the former case, if he had not been on this earthly plane during my lifetime, I would have continued to commune with this Soulmate energy on the inner plane or subjective realm.

STEP 13

Keeping Your Search
From The Inside Outward

Your Soulmate may not appear in your lifetime just because you are invoking the Universe for him or her. Do not physically search for your Soulmate. I did not do a single thing nor go to a single place with the express intent of physically searching for a mate. Some people get all dressed up and go out to various places trying to appear attractive. Trying to attract a mate in this way can be superficial.

Your search is from the inside outward. *A Soulmate connection is made by your inward journey not an outer one. It is about raising your vibration to bring about the attraction of your Soulmate to you.* You will meet when the time is right because he or she will naturally appear in your life space as you do the things you normally do.

Physically looking for your Soulmate may even hinder your progress because of your distraction from the real issue of developing yourself on the inside. What is in our consciousness will be outpictured in our outer world. To change our outer world we first change our inner reality. Our inner reality is reflected in our outer reality.

If we want a truly loving and spiritualized union with a mate we must imbue our own consciousness with this energy of thought, so that as we think, we realize and become.

MEDITATION

Turning The Search Light Within

I turn the search light inward.
I take the inward stroke
in order to know who I am.
I take the searchlight off others.

As I seek to know my own
Soul more intimately, I will come to
know more intimately the Soul of my mate.

STEP 14

Holding A Burning Desire

In invoking your Soulmate you must have *a deep desire and yearning for union* with this being in your life. This is not just a passing wish or fancy. For me, finding my Soulmate was a burning desire. You too must desire this event with all your heart, mind, body and soul. You consciously choose and desire this union above all others.

MEDITATION

Strong Spiritual Aspirations
And Desires On Your Journey

What are the strong spiritual aspirations
and lessons that capture your conscious
attention now in this lifetime?

Ask yourself, What are my burning desires
and where does union with a mate fit?

Is union with my Soulmate a strong
aspiration and a burning desire?

Energy, particularly sexual energy, is not flitted away
in relationships that hold no meaning to you. The Universe sees your need. However, if it appears that your
need is placated in casual sexual interaction with others, then the Universe does not see your urgency and
sincerity in truly aspiring to share your life fully with a
Soulmate. Thus, there is no need to grant you what you
say you really want.

You use and harness your life energy so that it becomes part of the magnetic and attractive power which
draws you and your Soulmate together. When our desire
is strong enough and we call out from the very depths of
our Soul for what we want and we are willing to sit with

the pain and empty hollow feeling as we await, then the Universe must pour forth in like measure that which we have asked for.

This process involves creating that place, or space, within your being to receive your gift of a Soulmate. This space may come to feel like a cavern, a hollow, empty space, but you must prepare such a place in order to receive. This place in you may also be experienced as an ache, as it did in me, but it is necessary. Nature abhors a vacuum and making room means making a place within to be fulfilled. Did you ever notice how some parents may better receive and may even love more the child they have made room for in their lives? Conversely, they may even come to feel burdened by the child they have not made room for in their lives.

Your whole being is moved by this aspiration or desire and must be made responsive and receptive to this event. Your Soulmate, that one whom you are divinely and perfectly suited for spiritually, mentally, emotionally, and physically may appear in a lifetime but this event does not occur in every lifetime.

On the other hand you may feel that finding your Soulmate may not be a focus in this lifetime. As such, you may lack this burning desire. You may have other spiritual aspirations and lessons to work on that capture your conscious attention.

It is important to move in accord with fulfilling your Soul's aspiration and what is right for your Soul's journey and expansion. Furthermore, a past lifetime union with your Soulmate may be so fresh in your memory that this is carrying you now in this lifetime. As such, there may be less desire on your part for this event in your life and more desire for other spiritual events and developments.

However, if this is a lifetime in which you find yourself strongly desiring union with your Soulmate, then ask the Universe for what you want. Pray your earnest prayers for this union. Even if he or she does not manifest in this lifetime, your earnest prayers, meditation, faith, and spiritual growth move you closer to the lifetime in which he or she will appear.

MEDITATION

**Is This The Lifetime
For Soulmate Union?**

Is this the lifetime in which both you
and your Soulmate are on the physical earth
plane at the same time?

How will you attract each other?
What series of events will unite
you on the earthly plane?
How many miles separate you spatially?
Perhaps he or she is right under
your nose and you fail to recognize him
or her at this point.

How will you recognize your Soulmate?

NOTES

Chapter Four

Listening To Spirit
For Inner Guidance—

Cultivating That Sacred Space
Within Through Prayer,
Meditation, and Invocation

August 15, 1984

Dear God, Father, Mother of My Soul,
I have felt and continue to feel lonely during this time. I wrote Jay a letter as a last resort telling him that I feel like a caged bird that is slowly dying. I ask him to love me so that I may sing again, or to let me go so that I may fly away. He has yet to respond to my letter.
It seems clear that he is unable to respond to me in the ways that I truly need. He completely does not know me. What can I say Lord? That leaves me to give up my expectations that he will change and fulfill my needs. Does this also mean that I give up my needs, my desires?
I seek spiritual, mental, emotional, and physical companionship. I love and want to serve you Father. Should I divorce?

STEP 15

Finding That
Sacred Space Within

One of the steps in invoking your union with your Soulmate is to have a deep communion with God, Goddess, Creator, Spirit, Higher Power, or however you *understand and call upon that force in, through and behind your life.* Cultivating and standing in that *sacred space within* is part of attuning and communing with the Master consciousness within you. How do you find and stand in that sacred space within you—that place where storms are not—that place that holds, nourishes, and sustains you?

August 15, 1984, continued ...

Oh God, tether me to Thee lest I stray.

Tethered here, I am anchored instead of buffeted by circumstance. In this place, I am able to transcend to higher spiritual realms. Sometimes you may catch a glimpse of the higher spiritual realms and your divine union with God. At those times you may feel lifted above the mundane worries of life and experience a sense of peace, ease and calm. You may experience a sense of well being in that everything is really okay. You may feel a sense of security. You may also experience a profound knowingness about the inner workings behind the Universe. This sense of comfort and knowingness becomes more and more of a backdrop to daily life, making daily challenges seem less of a burden and more of an opportunity.

You might ask yourself, What may I do to take this inward journey and strengthen this experience so that it is a part of every moment? Surely, in your immediate environment you have the experience of outwardly cultivating a space or place of comfort. Take your home for example. There you cultivate a space to inhabit. You sweep the floor, put a throw rug down, and light a fire in the fireplace.

Yet what have you been doing to cultivate this place, this space within you? Are you sweeping the floor within, are you tending the spirit, the sacred flame within you? By going inward through prayer and meditation, you increase your awareness of this flame within you. By bringing your awareness within, this flame grows and glows, radiating your whole being. As you bathe in this light through your daily practice of prayer and meditation you are then able to infuse this light into your daily activities, bringing this light out into the world around you.

MEDITATION

Strengthening Your Spiritual Connection

Ask yourself, What is my relationship
with God, Goddess, Spirit, Higher Power,
Creator, Energy or whatever way you
define your essence?
How might I strengthen this relationship?

Cultivating that place within is serious business. I once wrote a poem that tried to locate that place within me. This may sound silly, in the sense that this place is not physically locatable in time and space. Nevertheless, there is a seriousness in cultivating this place that deserves attention.

As you read the poem that follows, imagine yourself going deep within.

> **God Within,**
> **At the end of the depths of my eyes**
> **Beyond the thudding in my brain**
> **Down from the stuttering of my tongue**
> **Underneath the lump in my throat**
> **Past the heavy rising of my lungs**
> **Behind the pounding of my heart and**
> **the hollow of my stomach**
> **Somewhere along my spinal column**
> **There is a place where I go**
> **And I am with God.**

There is a place deep within you. In this place we come to recognize that God is our Eternal Friend and companion. Throughout our many lifetimes we have had many mothers, fathers, sisters, brothers and mates.

This relationship with The Absolute supersedes all others. It is the most enduring, never ending, unfailing, always present, always loving, always wise, always protective, always giving, near as the breath you feel on your top lip, this is how always near God, Goddess is and remains when others have departed from us.

MEDITATION

Your Eternal Oneness With Spirit

Imagine lying in bed at night
and hitting the rewind button on your day
and processing the day's events.
This is the Observer who stands
in back of the drama of life.
This is the knower or witness
who is extracting the essence of each
daily lesson that one day of living brings.

Now imagine laying in bed and closing your
physical eyes for a final time as you move
through the portal of life to afterlife.
Imagine having this same awakened
consciousness, that Observer and eternal
knower, that now hits the rewind button
on your entire lifetime.

The Observer is now extracting the
essence from the life's lessons which have
been garnered during your whole lifetime.

This observer then makes preparation
and seeks correct circumstances to again
take form, embarking on a new journey,
a new lifetime, in the whole cycle
of birth and rebirth.

Within this lifetime you are aware of your mortality. Yet as you become aware of the succession of lifetimes that you have lived as well as the spaces in between these lifetimes you are able to glimpse your immortality. Rather than isolate your awareness within any particular lifetime, you can bring your awareness to the continuous stream—your uninterrupted, eternal connection with God. *You are a part of this Great Cosmic Dance. Let yourself be lifted to an awareness of the spiritual realms!*

August 26, 1984, a.m.

Dear God,
I tried once again to talk with Jay. He says he does not think about our relationship. It is so hard to work with someone who will not think about our relationship, will not try to make it different and will not suggest how to end it!
I suggested that it is time for us to separate to which he responded, "Do what you want."
We are so disconnected. Together we have been like two musical instruments each melodious in our own turn, yet a cacophony of noise when we sought to play together—our sound grating on the nerves of the other.

We know when we are out of harmony with the energy vibration of another. I felt devoid of emotion at this point in our relationship. Try as we might over the many years, we just seemed to keep clashing in the same old ways.

STEP 16

Giving Appreciation
For Life And Living

August 26, 1984, continued ...

Dear God, Father of My Soul,
    I am truly thankful for all your bless-
ings. Health, beautiful children, a place to
rest after the day's work is done, nourish-
ment for the body and soul, family and
friends, and an inner radiance which
comes from keeping my heart, mind and
soul on you.

I would continually give thanks, praise and appreciation for my life and for all the many blessings God was
bestowing upon me. I experienced a joyfulness at my
core even in the midst of stormy situations.

STEP 17

Recognizing That Although You Are Lonely You Are Never Alone— The Loneliness And The Longing For Soulmate Union

August 31, 1984

Dear God,
My loneliness continues. I am trying to understand this feeling, trying to live with it, trying to get beyond it. But it is as a thorn in my side, a boulder on the road ahead, a lump in my throat.

I feel so lonely. It is an ache, a throb, a pain that does not cease. I say recitations of letting go. "Jay, I let go of my expectations that you will know me and be able to communicate with me in spiritual, mental and emotional ways."

I make an important distinction between the feeling of being lonely and being alone. Although I had to manage tremendous feelings of loneliness, I did not feel alone. I felt the presence and comfort of God's love at all times and I felt centered within my being.

August 31, 1984, continued ...

I now think constantly about my Soulmate. It may be a waste of time to do so. Why this unshakable loneliness and longing?

Is loneliness like fear, a feeling to be mowed down and conquered? If faith and courage are the antidote to fear then what is the antidote to loneliness? Lord, help me to conquer my loneliness.

It has helped me to re-read the Initiation during this time. In this book Elizabeth Haitch writes: "I did not know that this condition, in which a person feels as if he were in a desert crying from the depths of his soul for help, is the forerunner of salvation." [7]

I must go on, act as if God has granted my desire for perfect Soul and body union with my Soulmate.

Father, you know the depths of my loneliness and my desire to be with my spiritual and physical compliment, my Soulmate. But your will be done. I ask that you give me the strength to continue along the path whether this be part of my life or not.

STEP 18

Invoking The Universe
For What You Want

Even though God knows our hearts we have the responsibility to pray our earnest prayer, asking for what we desire and yet at the same time living in perfect peace with whatever the outcome. Invoking means to ask for what we want.

You must ask from the depths of your heart and soul. In this way what is asked is more likely to be in alignment with what God has already willed for your life. You must ask with purity and sincerity of heart. Then, as you will see in the chapters that follow, you must have the fortitude and the courage to remove anything within you that may act as a blockage to the receipt of your good—your gift of Soulmate Union.

PRAYER

A Prayer To Be United
With Your Soulmate

Dear God, I ask that you unite me
with my Soulmate—that one who is perfectly
and divinely suited for me spiritually,
mentally, emotionally, and physically.

That together we take away the longing
and loneliness, foster a deep, abiding sense
of fulfillment and enhance the expression
of the life purpose in one another.

January 16, 1985

Dear God, Father, Mother of My Soul,
The feelings now on the eve of seeing a
lawyer are the same. ... I long for love and
understanding. I desire harmony, peace, a
loving smile, a touch on the shoulder, yet
these are not forthcoming.
Of what has it benefited me to know
and feel the visions of such and to not
know their fulfillment? Of what has it
benefited me to see the heavens above yet
dwell in a box?

STEP 19

Holding The Vision
Of What You Want

Spirit blessed me with the vision of union with my Soulmate. This vision did not always feel like a blessing, yet it revealed to me the next steps that I was to follow. Without this vision I could not have been moved in the direction of my Soulmate.

Did you ever notice that while walking or driving a car that if your eyes begin to focus upon something your whole body begins to orient itself in the direction of where your eyes are looking? We must see or visualize what we want in order to create a new reality. Do not allow your current reality to blind your vision for your joyous union with your Soulmate.

By your outlook you shape your outcome. Golden strands of living, loving light issue forth when we visualize. These strands become the scaffolding of what we desire so that it may come into full manifestation. Our visualization becomes the webwork, the design, which in due time takes full expression.

STEP 20

Keeping The Faith

Your faith and spiritual connection helps you in your search in finding your Soulmate. In invoking the universe it is important to have faith that what you ask for is already done, then letting go and letting God.

If we plant an apple seed then we must wait, living in complete faith that only an apple tree will grow. We don't dig up the seed to see if growth is occurring nor doubt by thinking that the apple seed will suddenly grow into a pear tree.

We have faith that our invocation or call to God is heard and will be met with a response or evocation. We have faith that our prayers will be answered. We continue to be of service in the world, not because we are assured that what we ask for in faith will be given but because our first love and devotion is to God and that we are accepting of whatever God wills for our lives.

February 10, 1985

Dear God,
It is so refreshing and inspiring to re-read entries written in my journal from 1981, regarding my relationship with Jay. These speak of essentially the same frustrations I have at the present. The wisdom and integration I see here reveals to me where I have come from and where I need to go.

Rereading my journals at that time was like a *jolt* in awakening me to see in black and white, through the innocence of my own journal entries, how stuck I really was in my relationship. Entry after entry spoke of the same scenarios, the same disappointments, the same frustrations in communication.

In my desperation to improve the relationship, I had said to Jay a million times, "Let's try this", and "let's try that." *I could hardly believe how much I sounded like a broken record, as I poured out almost word for word, from one year to the next, the exact same concerns about a faltering relationship.*

Despite the efforts that both of us had made, the relationship had not been working. Furthermore, it was clearly evident in that moment that the relationship had not been working for years! But I could neither see nor accept this until now.

Jay and I made a mutual decision to separate that coming July of 1985, after having been together seventeen years. Yet, long before this day, I had spent many years in quiet contemplation of my Soulmate even while still in my marriage.

After the decision to separate was finally made my desire for union with my Soulmate intensified and *I prayed incessantly for him.* I had always asked God's help in life. I knew God would help me with finding my Soulmate.

STEP 21

Accepting Yourself As
A Spiritual Being—
Communing With God Continually

As a holistic psychotherapist I often ask clients, "What is going on for you spiritually and how is your faith helping you in your life challenge?" So often their answer is, "Well I have not been to church lately." What this usually means is: Because I have not been to a religious structure lately, I cannot embrace who I am as a spiritual being, nor do I feel validated in doing so.

I respond by saying, "Who we are as spiritual beings may be expressed within a particular structure such as a church or a temple, through a body of religious beliefs and observances, and in fellowship with others. However, *we are spiritual beings* right here and now, and we need not necessarily go to a particular religious structure to embrace ourselves as such. We are spiritual beings driving in our cars or washing the dishes.

In the very moment we find ourselves, we may commune and strengthen our connection with our Higher, God or Master consciousness. *Do not put off communing with God until you are within some religious structure. Your temple of God is within you.*"

It is important to make some distinction between religion and spirituality for many reasons—the aforementioned one in particular. To make this distinction I share the following story:

There once was a pond with lots of lily pads floating on the surface. (These lily pads represent the different religions.) A frog was spending considerable time rummaging around on his lily pad, extracting the experience, wisdom and essence therein.

As he sat perched on his own lily pad, he noticed all the warring that was going on between the various other lily pads, including his own. This resulted as the frog members from each of the lily pads all claimed to know the truth and to be the better lily pad (religion) over all of the others. He observed this peculiar behavior even among the frog members on his own particular lily pad. For some time thereafter, the frog continued in his studies and exploration of his own lily pad while continuing to take notice of the goings on between the other lily pads, in their constant bickering back and forth upon the pond's surface.

One day the frog decided to venture out to study and explore what was going on upon the other lily pads. This occurred much to the consternation of his fellow lily pad members who warned him terrible things would happen and bid him return back. The frog felt none of their inhibition or concern. So he leaped across the pond's surface, spending time on one lily pad then moving onto another. While rummaging around upon the other lily pads, this frog soon gained great insights from each one. A curious thing soon happened: he found a similar wisdom and essence on each lily pad and a resonance between them. Thus he expanded his own awareness.

Having gained this greater awareness and no longer feeling fastened to any one particular lily pad, this frog then decided to leap fully into the pond in order to experience the depths of the waters (spirituality) below. He soon discovered from this dual vantage point, of looking across the pond's surface as well as beneath to its depths, that he could now see and grasp that which is common and unifying for all lily pads. He knew these depths (spirituality) to be the water of spirit which is the underlying unity embracing all the diversity in its outward expression in the many lily pads above.

From this wonderfully all inclusive, all expansive, all sustaining and life giving spiritual essence he could feel his divine and infinite connection with all beings and all things. He was free to just be submerged in the waters of spirit. From this depth of awareness, he was also free to bobble up at any point, to any one lily pad or religious structure to experience its wisdom and essence. The frog was now free to express the unity he felt with all beings, through ritual and in sharing fellowship with others—thus infusing spirit into religion and expressing religion as living spirit.

Sometimes we stay on our lily pads beyond the point of benefit instead of exploring the variety and depth all around us. Whatever 'structure' we may choose it must serve as a vehicle for us to expand and grow, and not become a place of confinement.

Sometimes people feel that unless they are in a physical structure called a church, temple or religious organization, they cannot or do not feel their connection with God, Creator, Spirit, Life force, Higher Power, Master Consciousness, and so on. Others may feel alienated from or have little experience or connection with any particular religious structure or organization. Take time to create that church, temple, that *Sacred Space within You.* Then, it is always with you.

MEDITATION/PRAYER

Take Time Now
To Meditate Or Pray

Take time to pray or meditate
in your home, office or wherever
you are now standing or sitting.

You may begin simply by
giving thanks and appreciation
for just being alive,
or by asking for strength
and guidance in managing
the challenges in this day.

STEP 22

Creating That Outer
Sacred Space(s)

In addition to creating that sacred space within, also create an *outer physical space*, one in which you may easily enter daily to pray and meditate. This space may be in your home, office, or car for example. You make this space sacred by your prayers, meditation and daily reverence for life.

In this space you may have a favorite chair or floor cushions you sit upon. Add items that have a special meaning to you such as candles, incense, crystals, or inspirational readings. If you prefer, you might play music that is soothing and comforting.

As you use this space for prayer and meditation you imbue it with a sacred quality. Whenever you enter this outer Sacred space you will enliven your inner connection with God, giving you a sense of peace, ease, and security. Creating such a space(s) outside helps you to more easily go inward.

EXERCISE

Creating An Outer
Sacred Space

Take time to create an outer space
that is made sacred by your care,
meditations and prayers.

Think of how you will
arrange this space
and then implement
your plan.

Bless your space by offering this prayer (or one of
your own):

PRAYER

Blessing Your Sacred Space

May this space be one of the many spaces
that are touchstones for grounding the
divine energies that come through me
during my prayers and meditations.

May this space be filled with
Divine Light, Love, Wisdom and Power.
(In your mind's eye see this space as filled—
every crack and crevice, top to bottom, north,
east, south and west—with this Divine Light).

May a company of Divine Heavenly Angels
join me in this space to offer their
love, protection and guidance.
May this space be a place which aids me
to feel centered and at peace.
Thus, may I be rendered more capable
of fulfilling my work in the world.

—In Light, So May It Be.

NOTES

Chapter Five

Is There A Soulmate In Your Current Relationship?

STEP 23

Seeking To Unveil The Soulmate In Your Current Relationship— Doing The Hard Work Of Relationship Building

---

Entire books could be written about this step which is included here as just one chapter. Take a moment to appreciate that whoever your current mate is, the two of you have been brought together for a purpose. *There is no accident in your meeting.* You are attracted to one another because what you share together holds some key to your unfoldment as you journey together.

Lester and I have found that even being in a Soulmate union requires hard work and skill. We seek to know one another more and more deeply so we must work through those issues that would potentially hinder our goal. Some of the most important ingredients to a successful union are:

1. **Commitment**
2. **Connection**
3. **Communication**
4. **Conflict Resolution Skills**
5. **Caring Contact and Intimacy**

1. COMMITMENT

1. Generally when two people who love each other and are romantically involved think of commitment they may think about staying together over time, sharing their lives as friends, lovers, parents and even coworkers, and forsaking all others. However, there is more to the story of commitment.

One aspect of commitment is that both mates remain actively committed to their own Soul's growth and evolving. Each mate does their own hard work of self discovery, self healing and self unfolding. Each mate seeks to self actualize and to be the best that he or she can be. Each mate works to develop their spiritual gifts so that they may uplift themselves and their union, and then work to make the world a better place.

Couples will often experience difficulty in their union when one mate is working harder on self discovery and improvement than the other. The union can become strained when one or both mates stop trying to make needed self improvements. In the play, 'How to Love A Black Woman,' one of the male actors is staggering around intoxicated as he laments how much he loves his Black Woman. He explains, "But she wants me to change. I say, change from what to what?"

When I would beseech my first husband to consider making needed changes in himself and in our relationship he would maintain that he was like he was when I met him and that he was not going to start changing now. This kind of attitude can create stagnation in a committed relationship.

Both mates must remain in a lifelong commitment to do the inner work. The life urge within you both is ever propelling you to greater levels of awareness. If this urge is harnessed the union may prosper and grow. Furthermore, the union itself has life. It lives and breaths and must continually be vitalized by the concerted efforts of each mate. Many steps of self discovery are outlined in this book. A wealth of information is also available today on self help and relationship building to help you in this process.

2. Another aspect of commitment is that both mates remain actively committed to promoting the Soul growth of their mate. This means that both mates sincerely make and uphold a pledge to help one another to live and express their fullest potential. It also means trusting one another and the power of the Absolute that is animating your lives as a couple.

At times one mate may worry that if he supports his mate to develop particular strengths that she may no longer need him. These kinds of preoccupations can create a withholding of the loving and transformative energy that is needed to keep the relationship alive. A husband (or wife) may even withhold complimenting his mate out of fear that to fully honor all that she is evolving to be may put him at risk in some way. He (she) may feel threatened by the fact that his mate is growing stronger, more beautiful, more confident and more radiant in the light.

Couples must commit to promoting the greatest good in one another even if it means they should part, letting one another go.

AFFIRMATION

Sharing My Spiritual Gifts

I do my best to promote the
greatest good in my mate.
This means I share the insights
and spiritual gifts that I have been
given with him or her.

If my mate should
choose to leave the relationship,
I release him or her to do so,
but I freely give my spiritual gifts, unafraid.

I release any and all fears.
I greet my mate's unfolding
with a spirit of awe and joy.

It is important that a couple is working in a Spirit of
goodwill. To accomplish this a mutual exchange must
take place in which each partner freely gives their insight, urgings, support and feedback to his or her mate
and receives these in return. Both mates agree to try on
the feedback that is given in a spirit of nondefensiveness.
The mate trying on the feedback opens to the idea that
what has been offered may hold insight and information
that will guide or indicate the next spiritual step to be

taken. When viewed this way the insights that your mate gives can be seen as spiritual gifts or messages and received with a spirit of gratitude.

Your mate is that being that you spend much of your life with on earth. He or she is there to reflect who you are becoming and to mirror your progress along the way. There is a seemingly endless list of qualities that your mate may be helping you to unfold at any given time. This list may include becoming more sensitive, asser-tive, patient, courageous, disciplined, responsible, and creative, just to name a few.

EXERCISE

Helping Your Mate To Unfold His Or Her Spiritual Gifts

Offer your support, insights and spiritual gifts
to him or her unconditionally.
As you do so, it may sound like this:

I have noticed that it has been hard for you to be more assertive. (Give your mate one or more examples of when you noted that this quality of assertiveness was under expressed.) Being more assertive is something you may want to learn more about at some point in your journey, in this life or in the next. If you are willing, I want to help you to unfold this quality within you. I will share with you what I have learned so far in my journey about being more asser-

tive in the hope that it will help you. Perhaps this is something I have come to teach you just as you have also come to teach me how to be more _____(fill in the blank with whatever quality you are cultivating such as being more open, economical, organized, etc.). Now of course you may choose whether or not to learn more about this valuable life lesson with me or with someone else, now or in the future. Is this something that you choose to do with me at this time? The choice is yours.

3. This next aspect of commitment is related to the previously mentioned Step 8, Keeping Your Focus On The Light: Keeping God First In Your Life. This means that both mates remain committed to the growth of divine light in their union as a couple. At times one or both partners may feel spiritually disconnected and out of contact with their God Power or Spiritual Essence.

Cultivating a daily practice of tapping into this boundless source allows both mates to draw from this fount for renewed insight, strength and guidance in intelligent living. This Light or Universal Power heals and restores. When this connection is absent mates may feel depleted. They will siphon off energy from one another and thus begin to deplete the relationship as well. Even though they may still attend to the immediate needs of the home and family they may have stopped attuning to the Spiritual Essence or Divine Light within one another and their union.

As a couple, it is critical that you seek to understand this Divine Light in yourself, your mate and in your union. It is almost impossible to truly see it in your union without seeing it in yourself and in your mate first. As you orient yourselves in this way to this Divine Light, it acts as a beacon drawing you forward, bringing clarity of purpose to your relationship, steadying and coordinating your footsteps together as a couple on the path of return to God. Your union opens more to rendering itself as a vessel for Spirit to work through.

This kind of orientation in your union helps you to see more clearly how to fulfill your work together in the Great Divine Plan on earth. What a joyous journey this can be!

2. CONNECTION

This means connecting with one another physically, emotionally, mentally, and spiritually. It is the magnetism and resonance between mates. Connection is the compatibility couples have in their energy makeups. There is more of a match between them as each brings qualities of energy that compliment and blend well together in the union. [8] These qualities support the life work that each has come to do. Even if two people feel connected to each other in one or two of these planes, they may grow to feel more connection on all four planes over time. [9]

For example a couple may initially feel physically and emotionally connected. They may work together to grow and connect more mentally and spiritually. This growth may occur as they share more in one anothers world view, talk more about their ideas about life and come to see more clearly from one anothers perspective.

Couples grow together more spiritually as they awaken more to the divinity and sacredness of their own being. As one partner takes that inward stroke and seeks to know himself more fully physically, emotionally, mentally and spiritually he will learn more about connecting with his mate in these ways. As he awakens more to his own God Self and God qualities he will likewise yearn for and seek out the divinity and God qualities in his mate.

Things can come up in a union that temporarily interfere with a couple's ability to connect physically, emotionally, mentally, and spiritually. However, as you continue to work together you may discover that what originally felt like a non-Soulmate union becomes a Soulmate union. Just holding the vision and seeing the potential for connecting more fully can help couples cultivate or recapture the communication they need to help them to continue unfolding together as spiritual beings.

As a couple is growing toward one another and working to strengthen their connection they will meet each others needs more fully and successfully. As both partners do the inner spiritual work they may find that they become more attuned and in harmony with themselves and subsequently with their mate. You will begin to experience yourselves more as Souls with a Universal purpose.

This Universal purpose has the power to re-focus the mundane concerns of life so that these weigh you down less, causing less interference in your union. Your daily anxieties and concerns wane as your vision together grows. It becomes more evident that your coming together is much larger than the two of you. A new vista of meaning and purpose in your lives together will begin to emerge.

3. COMMUNICATION

Communication is vital in a relationship. *Communication is the life energy in a relationship—it nourishes the relationship.* When communication is cut off in a relationship a kind of death sets in, just as if circulation were cut off to a limb.

When couples engage in arguing where tempers are flaring no real communication is taking place. This is demonstrated over and over in couples therapy, as couples are unable to hear one another and are even unable to hear themselves as they say things that they later can not remember having said. Often, following these conflicts, couples withdraw into angry silences, without speaking to one another for days, weeks or even months— again with no real communication taking place. If a couple averages one week per month of no or strained communication, they may lose up to three months per year of communication time in the relationship. This is long time to go without circulation! It is time lost in nurturing the life of the union.

In referring to **Diagram 1,** (see the following page) the center of the circle or the bull's eye represents stage one in communication when the couple is really connecting and in alignment with one another; they are in a 'groove' and 'getting along.' They are communicating, checking in with one another, processing their day together and inquiring about one anothers well being. They are talking about how they are doing currently as a couple and they are creating and discussing their vision for the future. They work cooperatively in their common purpose, taking care of home, family and so on. They express caring contact and are sexually intimate with one another.

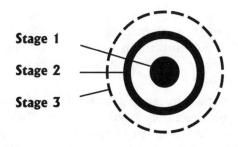

DIAGRAM 1

**Hitting the Target
in Communication**

The next ring represents the second stage when communication within the couple has cooled, becoming more distant. This change is generally due to some kind of conflict that has occurred in the relationship (although feeling rushed or fatigued may also be factors). The observed pattern is that couples will circumscribe their communication to include only those issues immediately related to the continued functioning of the house and the care of the children. One mate asks the other to bring home a loaf of bread or informs that the plumber is coming and needs to be let in at a set time. If a couple is nursing a sick child and one mate has given little Jimmy medicine the other is informed so that the medicine is not given twice or not at all. However, when communication deteriorates further even these things may go uncommunicated.

This is represented by the outer ring or third stage. A case example of this stage is of Thomas. He went to pick up the couple's daughter at daycare as he usually did each day. He discovered when he got there that his wife had picked up the child and never said a word about her plan to do so. Other examples include failure to communicate about nonpayment of bills or the status of the children. One mate may make a school or medical visit with a child and not communicate the outcome with their mate. In stage 3, the plumber comes to fix the leak and no one is home to let him in! Some couples report that the degree of deterioration in their communication places them even beyond the third ring in the diagram! Once the couple moves beyond the bull's eye there is generally little or no communication between them about how each is doing. The relationship is put on hold as couples steep in conflict about issues.

When couples communicate, they keep the relationship viable. Out of that viability comes the potential and opportunity for spiritual growth, change and unfoldment. This involves developing the ability to listen and to hear your mate, validating her being and responding to her empathically. If you began to hear strange sounds under the hood of your car or no sound at all you may ignore this problem for a day or so, but would soon seek a mechanic to make these needed repairs or adjustments. Similarly, when couples start hearing strange sounds or the absence of sound which comes as couples engage in angry silences then it is important to make needed repairs to the communication system in the relationship.

As a couple if you are unhappy with your patterns of communication, then make the necessary changes and seek assistance if necessary. As couples keep playing out the same unfulfilling patterns they will find that they will keep arriving at the same unfulfilling outcomes. Outcomes they do not feel good about. When a cue stick hits a pool ball, the ball has a certain progression, or path, which it will follow invariably unless there is an outside variable or intervention that changes or redirects its course. Similarly our patterns, like the pool ball, will run their course unless we are willing to make necessary changes. If you are unhappy with your patterns of relatedness and you want something different to happen in your relationship then you must do something different. It is that simple.

It is vital that a couple has the tools for enhancing their communication and that they understand some of the mechanics of good and effective communication. There are many. One of the firsts steps is spending quality time together communicating each day. Many things can effect the amount of time mates spend together like demanding work/career schedules and childrearing.

Nevertheless, couples will benefit from spending at least twenty minutes together (and more if possible) each day talking to one another. What couples talk about during this time may include the following recommended topics:

a. Processing your day with one another. This includes asking one another questions like: How was your day? How did the events of the day make you feel? What spiritual lessons are you learning from your daily challenges? This is an important time to soothe and comfort one another from the impacts of the day and to hear and validate one another's feelings. It is also an opportunity to problem solve together and offer insights and suggestions as to how each may better manage work, interpersonal issues, stress, and so on.

b. Talking about the couple or your union. These discussions may be titled, *Let's talk about Us*. This includes asking one another questions like: How do you feel about me? In what areas might I improve? What are some of the ways I may touch you more deeply and know you better? What have you been envisioning lately for our lives together?

c. Raising or revisiting issues that need to be worked through and resolved. (See next section.) Say to your mate, "Let's get back to the issue that came up this morning. I have had some additional thoughts and feelings about what we discussed that I would like to share with you in hope that it will add some clarity and the issue can move to a place of resolution."

4. CONFLICT RESOLUTION SKILLS

It is important that couples understand and use the energy of conflict resolution. Couples will benefit from developing the skills which aid them to feel more comfortable sitting with and working through the conflict that naturally arises in any relationship—even Soulmate relationships.

One system for understanding energy describes the energy of conflict resolution as the Fourth Ray of Harmony Through Conflict[10]. This is the energy of mediation, balance and restoring harmony. Finding harmony through conflict means *working through the conflict* not going to the left or to the right of it, or attempting to otherwise avoid it. Thus conflict is worked through en route to re-establishing the harmony.

One extreme or misuse of this energy is experienced as *Warring*. Both mates may be using this energy to war with one another. Probably everyone has known someone who has gone around stirring up all the problems and discord without a clue on how to fix or resolve the situation and maybe little concern in doing so.

They are sensitive to dissonance and easily tune into it. Mates who engage in this pattern find themselves at war for warring sake. They are habituated to the fight and lose sight of the goal which is to resolve the conflict and restore harmony. Even if they do not like the bad feelings that recur when they fight they are accustomed to these feelings and do not know the pathway to a better set of feelings when they interact.

A case example is of Michael and Marsha. Sparks would fly between them as both would bring up issue after issue each charging the other with being at fault. Both were unable to stay with one issue as one partner heard and validated the other for what he or she had just raised. As they engaged in warring, it was easy to see that when Michael raised an issue, instead of hearing him fully, Marsha was anxiously searching her memory bank for a counter issue to hurl back at Michael and vice versa.

At the other extreme, this energy, when misused is experienced as a kind of *Pseudo Peace*. An example of this is when you go to a manager or supervisor and outline areas to be problem solved. Your manager responds by cordially dismissing your concerns and essentially tells you to go back to work and "make nice." You walk away feeling not responded to. Similarly this energy may be expressed in a union as one or both mates avoid talking about issues or collude not to discuss things that will lead them to experience the tension that normally arises as they address issues.

A case example is of Dave and Linda who had been married fifteen years but came to couples therapy because neither felt their needs were getting met. The couple had a pattern of tiptoeing around conflict, which made it impossible for either to articulate there needs. They were of the belief that if you do not ask you do not get rejected. History revealed that both had grown up with parents that supported this kind of pattern. Dave had grown up with a father who battered his wife and had vowed he never wanted to treat his wife this way. He was commended in his effort to heal his life and not recreate his father's abusive pattern in his own relationship. However in his effort to avoid and steer clear of conflict he had gone to the other extreme, misuse of this Fourth Ray energy to create a Pseudo Peace in which issues rarely got resolved.

This couple thought it was better to have a Pseudo Peace than to be Warring. But both examples represent misuse of this energy. Pseudo peace is a mother who knows incest is going on in the family and says nothing in order to not blow the system. It is a manufacturing company where those in its employ know that faulty products are being sold to the public, but they keep silent so as not to rock the boat.

A good way to capture both extremes or misuses of this energy is by reflecting upon some of the injustices that have been done to people in the world. These abuses occur not simply because people have made war upon one another (Warring) but also because so called 'good people' said nothing (Pseudo Peace) and through their silence allowed conflict to go unaddressed and unresolved thus no true peace could result.

A couple can also be engaged in both a Warring and Pseudo Peace pattern of communication like in the case of Martin and Denise. Denise would constantly raise issues that needed to be addressed in the relationship. These issues involved the finances, inequitable patterns in role sharing and Martin's lack of attention to the relationship as he spent many hours out of the house. Martin on the other hand would put off Denise's requests for time to discuss these issues by watching TV, walking out of the house, or not coming home. During sessions Martin avoided issue by appearing bored or by flirting with Denise, trying to cajole her out of her insistence that these issues be addressed. He did not take these issues seriously. As Martin distanced and avoided more, Denise ranted, begged and pleaded more.

Men like Martin and Dave from the previous couple, frequently express an avoidance pattern for a variety of reasons. However, one predominant reason is they do not know how to enter into the conflict arena with the women they love in a way that feels skilled and safe for them both.

In referring to **Diagram 2,** the triangle is used as a symbol. The two extremes are represented by the base of the triangle with Warring at one extreme and Pseudo Peace at the other. The point of balance in finding harmony through conflict is represented by the apex.

Harmony Through Conflict

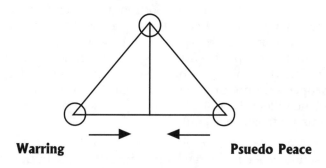

Warring   **Psuedo Peace**

DIAGRAM 2

Conflict Resolution

If W = Warring and P = Psuedo Peace, then couple combinations are as follows:

PP — Both mates are walking on eggshells, avoiding and unable to explore conflict.

WW — Both mates are arguing (fighting).

WP or PW — One partner is raising conflict issues and the other is avoiding these issues.

As couples develop the skills to move toward center and find balance between these extremes, they are able to work through the conflict and re-establish harmony as issues arise. It is important that couples enter into conflict with the goal of resolution. Couples need to acquire the tools to sit with, as well as express the emotions that arise. These strong emotions can effect how clearly two people are thinking as well as their ability to hear one another as they try to wade through issues.

Additionally, mates bring their histories from childhood and previous relationships to their unions. These histories may include angry and noncommuncative role models and patterns. If replicated in your union, these histories will cause similar kinds of unhappy interactions as the ones witnessed by you in earlier relationships. When couples lack the skill to sit with or to express anger (as well as other strong emotions) they may express aggressive communication patterns or may avoid conflict out of fear of loss of control. It is understandable how people have difficulty moving toward center. Many folks have grown up in families where they have seen one extreme use of this energy or the other. They have watched family members Warring with one another, avoiding issues in order to have a Pseudo Peace or a combination of both.

There will always be issues to resolve in the life of the couple. The issues just get different over time. What is important is that couples preserve their relationship despite the issues that arise from time to time creating conflict in the union. The relationship is the continuous stream that is enlarged by the attention and nurturing given to it by both mates. Issues are what happen on occasion in the relationship. They are the occasional blips on the screen in the ongoing and continuous stream of relationship.

However, for some couples this gets reversed. When that happens the couple experiences a continuous stream of issues with an occasional blip on the screen of relationship. When this kind of reversal occurs issues loom so large that they become the focus in the union instead of the relationship. When couples lack a mechanism in their communication repertoire for resolving conflict a rawness can occur as issues become the focus rather than the cultivation of the relationship.

Initial, Unresolved
Conflict Stage

Partial Resolution Stage

Full Conflict
Resolution Stage

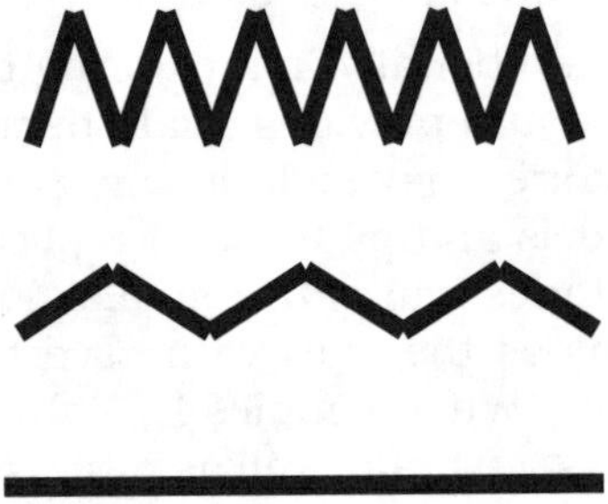

DIAGRAM 3

Stages in Conflict
Resolution Process

In referring to **Diagram 3,** the first wavy line represents the tension that can occur within the couple when an issue first arises. This is what I call Initial or Unresolved Conflict stage. It may happen as you are both getting yourselves and possibly children ready to leave for work (and school) in the morning. This is a time when emotions can run high as one or both feels invested in expressing their viewpoint. When an issue first arises I support couples to process and problem solve the issues as much as they can in the first sitting while validating one anothers feelings. Sometimes couples need to say, "Let's talk about this later tonight" because they are both running late. Sometimes emotions are running too high and couples need to take time out. A couple's ability to even hear one another may be hindered when emotions are highly charged.

Resolving conflict is a process. When conflict arises generally one mate will hold the emotional or anger charge for a longer time period than the other mate. This emotional charge may also include frustration, resentment, sadness, and so on. The mate who holds the emotional or anger charge longer will need a longer *Recovery Time* before coming to the table to discuss the issue while the other mate will feel ready to re-engage sooner. This is fine. In a similar manner, if both mates had the flu one would likely recover more quickly than the other. Each is a unique individual and is expected to differ from the other in a variety of ways. However, even if one mate recovers quicker from the flu it is the union that still has the 'flu' until both mates recover. The union is not recovered until both mates are recovered and harmony is restored to the union.

In your own union, take time to notice which mate generally needs a longer recovery time when conflict arises. Some couples are ready to re-engage after just minutes or hours. However in some couples the mate that holds the emotional or anger charge longer may take one to several days or even weeks before the emotions are more settled and there is a readiness to re-engage. I support this mate to shorten the interval to within a 24 hour period or less. Try to search inwardly to see what is going on inside and ask yourself if this could be worked through in a shorter interval so that you learn a quicker recovery time when conflict issues arise. Likewise it is important that your mate honor the need for recovery time and provide some space away from focusing on the issue so that this can take place.

A couple is supported to still have some affectionate contact with one another during this interval (see next section on Caring Contact) even while this issues remains unresolved. Remember, there will always be issues to resolve, that issues just get different over time, and that any one issue will be moving through various stages of resolution. A couple is not always able to resolve an issue in one sitting. I support couples to give up the idea that an issue will be resolved in one sitting. If it can be, fine, but this is not always the case. I ask couples to contract to revisit and re-discuss the issue within a twenty-four hour period.

This revisiting within a twenty-four period is represented by the second less wavy line in Diagram 3. As you can see, some tension reduction has occurred and this is called a Partial Resolution. During this time you and your mate have had a chance to replay in your own minds the feedback, observations, or argument earlier offered by the other. This allows both of you the opportunity to begin to see the issues from the other's perspective and to empathize with the other's feelings. Both of you have had a chance to think about and better understand the issue and to use this time to get on top of your emotional response.

As you and your mate now come back to the table and revisit the issue both of you have had time to think about what you will say in a way that does not raise defensiveness in your mate. You may also need to seek out additional information to bring back to the discussion which will help clarify the issues. As a couple you may need to revisit an issue two, three or several times before it is resolved and becomes a non-issue. Couples may find as they make subsequent passes in revisiting the issue that emotions or lack of clarity flare again causing a return to a previous level of conflict tension. Do not be discouraged—just continue trying to work through the issue—revisiting it within a twenty-four hour period.

When the couple has finally resolved the issue to the place where it becomes a non-issue harmony is achieved and a sense of balance or equilibrium is experienced. This is represented by the third, flat line in Diagram 3 where the couple has revisited the issue until it has been resolved. This is called the Full Conflict Resolution Stage. This flat line symbolizes the end of a process which then renders the fruit or essence of valuable learning. In this way couples have a way to sweep the slate clean so that unresolved conflict from issues does not accumulate in the union. When couples do the hard work of reaching this line this essence can be extracted and applied to future conflict to reduce tension and hasten the resolution process.

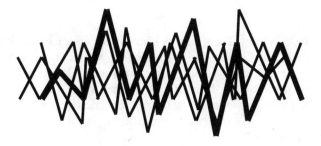

DIAGRAM 4

Wall in Communication

Diagram 4 shows the effects of what happens in communication when unresolved issues from the past are carried over into future discussions. These multiple commingled and commangled wavy lines represent the multiple issues that have been allowed to go unresolved. When this happens attempts to discuss current issues become frustrated and clouded. One mate may be trying to talk about the current issue as the other mate is bringing up unresolved issues from the past and interjecting them into the present discussion. Over time, if this kind of pattern continues a wall forms between two people that they feel cannot be scaled or penetrated.

DIAGRAM 5

**Building a Strong Foundation
in Communication**

In contrast, **Diagram 5** shows the effect of working through conflict to the point where it becomes a non-issue. In this way couples are gradually able to build a foundation which becomes a strong base for them to stand upon, instead of a wall which comes between them. If couples lack a contract for resolving issues, issues will go unresolved.

Today the issue is which mate left clothing strewn on the floor—tomorrow it is failing to pick the other up at the appointed time. Sometimes the issues are extremely serious and involve major violations of trust in the relationship, like infidelity. Even a seemingly small issue involving one mate failing to perform a task or duty as promised may stir up deep childhood wounds in the other mate who grew up not being able to trust and depend on her caregivers. Issues, whether seemingly large or small need to be addressed or else they would not have arisen in the relationship in the first place. Angry outbursts, withdrawal, distancing, and withholding of affection are all symptoms of lacking conflict resolution skills. I support couples to both read on their own and to do couples therapy to aid their understanding of the mechanics of communication that foster restoration of harmony and true peace in their union.

5. CARING CONTACT/INTIMACY

Caring contact includes the way couples show affection for one another. This involves some touch or skin to skin contact in which mates kiss, hug, hold hands, massage one another, and so on. At times, this touch may culminate in arousal or sexual expression, but is not necessarily the intention. The intention is to say to your mate, "I care." I support couples to develop and express both affectionate and sexual touch. Some men will find it difficult to cultivate their touch to say, I care, without it being goal directed to having sex. Practice will help.

A case is Monique and Jason. Monique would complain that Jason did not show her enough affection and when he would touch her his touch was sexualized—directed to her breasts or buttocks. It is important that men learn how to hug their mates at times the same way they would hug their mother or a dear friend, in a way that just says, "I have the highest regard for you and I care."

When couples lack a contract for resolving issues they experience frequent interruptions in their caring contact and intimacy. A little math again reveals that they may go days, weeks or months without kissing, embracing or having sexual intercourse. I support couples to have at least two caring/affectionate contacts per day (and more) in spite of the fact that they may still have some issues that have as yet to be resolved. Remember that in having a contract to revisit the issues within a 24 hour period, again taking opportunity to work through conflict, you keep activated a mechanism for conflict resolution. When this contract is in place it allows you to stay in the stream of relationship with your mate in the midst of resolving the issues that naturally arise.

So much is communicated through touch. The skin is the largest organ in the body. When you touch your mate you keep a link with him enlivened and the healing energy of love is allowed to circulate within the union, thus vitalizing it. Sometimes couples will stand far apart as they give one another a small peck on the lips because their is still some residual conflict to be resolved. This is okay. What is important is that couples maintain some skin contact even in the midst of problem solving.

Some women are particularly resistant to the suggestion that affectionate contact remain uninterrupted even in the midst of trying to resolve conflict. A woman may feel that the idea of continuing to hug or kiss her mate through this process somehow compromises her or communicates to the mate that he has been 'let off the hook' regarding the resolution of the issues that are on the table. To the contrary, continuing to kiss and embrace in the midst of problem solving communicates that you care about the relationship and that you are able to put the issues in their proper perspective.

Men I see in couples work are particularly affected by the withholding of affection by their mates and really need this contact. This contact says to them, "I love you while you are in process." Remember, that if you know that issues will be brought back to the table in a 24 hour period you will relax more which will allow the continual flow of caring contact. Cultivate the practice of bringing issues back to the table within a 24 hour period and continuing to express affection for one another.

You will actually find that it is the continuous flow of love between the two of you that butters the communication mechanism and keeps it all working. This touch is unconditional. The fact that this kind of caring contact happens even after you and your mate have had some conflict is a testimonial of your love and regard for one another.

This kind of love is a reflection of the love God has for you. Divine Love enfolds you even in the midst of your seeming imperfection, when you are out of harmony in relationship to yourself, your mate, your community or even the Universe. This Divine Love is never withheld from you or cutoff. This is one of the many ways we more approximate God's love for us by continuing to love and make caring contact with our mate even when we feel hurt, anger or displeasure.

EXERCISE

A Pledge To Our Union

At the conclusion of a seven week couple's group, which allows couple's to honor the sacredness of their union and their journey together, and to enhance their communication, I ask them to make the following pledge to one another.

Meditate upon it with your mate asking how it may be adapted in your own lives.

<u>A PLEDGE TO OUR UNION</u>

- *We accept that we need to create new patterns of communicating with one another.*

- *We are willing to do the hard work of improving communication and agree to try on new ways of relating in order to improve, preserve and enhance our union.*

- *We agree to unfold the Highest and Greatest Good in one another. We approach one another always in a Spirit of Goodwill and Helpfulness. We have a genuine interest in and work hard to promote the Spiritual Growth of one another.*

- *We will spend quality time each day talking to one another, which will include talking about the relationship, 'Us' as a couple. We agree to listen to one another even when we disagree.*

- *We acknowledge that their will always be issues to be resolved as part of living and that the issues just get different over time.*

- *We agree to keep the relationship the focus and not the issues. We agree to cultivate the continuous stream of relationship, resolving the intermittent blips of issues that occur on this con-tinuous stream of relationship versus cultivating a continuous stream of issues with only an occasional blip of relationship between us.*

- *We will work to resolve any conflict that comes up in our relationship without engaging in a 'Warring' (confused combativeness) or 'Pseudo Peace' (covering over, denial of issues). We seek to restore the balance and harmony that comes from working through the conflict in order to know true peace in our union.*

- *When an issue arises, we agree to process it as much as we can to try to resolve it.*

- *If we are unable to resolve the issue, we agree to revisit those unresolved conflict areas within a 24 hour period and to continue to process them to the point of resolution.*

- *We let go of the expectation that the issues that arise will be resolved in one sitting. If they can be resolved in one sitting we will do so.*

- *We understand that we may have to revisit an issue 2, 3 or many times before it is finally resolved and becomes a non-issue.*

- *We agree to cultivating a more rapid recovery time from our emotional charge over the conflict that has arisen. We will shorten the interval between being angry with one another and getting back to Stage 1 communication.*

- *We will not seek the 'who is the most injured award.' Nor do we seek to 'score' in an argument, thus winning over one another. Instead we seek a victory for the unity and integrity of the relationship. Winning means doing what brings us closer together and strengthens us as a couple.*

- *We will not allow conflict to interfere with our display of affection for one another.*

- *We will continue to be affectionate and intimate with one another as we experience and work through periods of conflict resolution.*

- *We will not let more than 24 hours go by in which we are not communicating and displaying affection for one another.*

- *We agree to at least two skin-to-skin contacts each day, i. e., hugs, kisses, massages, hand holding, and so on.*

- *When we need 'down time' from communicating we will declare a 'time out' for a specified period of time.*

- *I will stay in my mastery and abide by this agreement and uphold this pledge for the sake of our union even at those times when my mate does not, trusting that my mate will do the same for the union, when I falter.*

- *I will regard this pledge as a sacred agreement between my Higher Consciousness and my mate.*

- *I will not destroy this pledge in a moment of anger.*

Couple's signature   *Date:*

Prepared by: Terri Nelson, L.I.C.SW., M.S.W., M.S.E.P.

I have found in my work with couples that they are generally in one of three positions along a continuum when they come in for couples counseling:

1. The first position is that a couple wants to use therapy to try on new ways of being to improve, enhance and preserve the union. They are interested in gaining insights and acquiring the tools that will aid them to make necessary changes. I strongly support couples to preserve, enhance, and improve their unions.

2. The second position is that they are straddling the fence. They have one foot in the marriage or union and one foot out. They want to use therapy to help them decide whether to renew and reinvest their energies in the relationship or whether they should begin to invest their energies in another direction.

3. The third position is that a couple has already decided to separate and end the relationship but wish to use therapy to transform their relationship from one that has previously been romantic and sexual to one that is not necessarily friends (although this may be the case), but is friendly enough so that they may continue to co-parent children, continue as co-workers, agree on division of assets, or to respond cordially if they see each other in public or other settings.

It is easy to see from the above that different combinations may arise in that one mate may be in the first position of wanting to work to improve the relationship while the other is in the second position of straddling the fence, and so on. In therapy couples will often talk about how they almost walked away from each other. Later they realized that as they continued the hard work of communication and relationship building whole new chapters of meaning and purpose in their journey together began to reveal themselves. This new depth of commitment, purpose, love, Soul connection and direction was the fruitage of their earlier struggles which they may now harvest together as they continue their journey as a couple.

Do the hard work of relationship building in the hope of unveiling the Soulmate in your current relationship. If Spirit is guiding you to stay and work through the struggles, then listen!

STEP 24

Letting Go And
Releasing In Relationships

Sometimes in relationships there is the recognition that your paths are moving in different directions and there comes a time of parting.

After many years of struggle and frustration, I knew that my first marriage was coming to an end. Although we did try therapy, it was much too brief and came much too late in the process. We now needed to release one another from the bonds that had joined us—bonds that had formed between us over the course of our long-term relationship. I had pained and agonized for several years but arrived at a point wherein I knew letting go was absolutely necessary for my spiritual well being. I began to say recitations daily to effect this change. I would say:

> *I loose you Jay, I let you go, I release*
> *you to your greatest and highest good. You*
> *are free. May you go in peace. You loose*
> *me, you let me go, you release me to my*
> *greatest and highest good. I am free. May I*
> *go in peace.*

Letting go in relationships is an important step. Think of all the love songs that are binding in nature in what they affirm: "Oh baby you are going to be mine forever and ever." Almost every radio station chants these songs. We see and feel the sway and attractive power of these *words* to create bonds between two people. Yet we also need to use the power of the word in letting go and releasing in relationships! *It is important to do recitations to let go and to release.*

A tremendous amount of energy goes into the bonds that are created between two people. By becoming unbound we free and release that energy so that it may seek other unions. This energy becomes an attractive force enabling us to connect in a new relationship. Dr. Scott Peck in his book, The Road Less Traveled says, "LOVE is promoting the spiritual growth of oneself and the other even if it means letting the other go." [11]

Sometimes it becomes necessary for two people who have been in a romantic union to let each other go and wish each other well on their spiritual paths. Jay and I were unhappy together and *I realized that letting him go was to continue to love and promote him spiritually.* We may stay in a relationship that we know is not serving our own or our mate's highest good not out of love but out of fear, guilt, insecurity and so on. We may leave a relationship out of love and a sincere desire to foster the spiritual well being of our mate and ourselves.

In doing couples therapy, I often observe that tension arises when partners have either stopped working together or one partner feels that he or she is doing more of the work in the relationship than the other. There is an unevenness in the amount and quality of energy that each contributes to the relationship. Often there is a lot of effort expended by both mates but it is energy of miscommunication, anger, and conflict over differing goals.

Differences in the qualities of energy that each partner brings to the relationship can lead to disharmony despite continued efforts to live and work together, harmoniously. Defining their life purpose and work together and how this is to be accomplished continues to elude them. Sometimes you can't 'fix' a relationship just because you want to especially if you feel you are trying to do so all by yourself. Sometimes couples simply find that they are not going in the same direction. This was all true of my relationship.

More painful is the dawning awareness among couples that they may not have an enduring mission to continue as romantically involved partners, working purposely together in this earthly incarnation. Working together means maintaining the commitment to unfold the Soul. This means that each mate promotes the growth of their own Soul and the Soul of their mate. Accomplishing this sometimes means an enduring relationship or it may mean letting each other go.

Today, people are moving beyond staying in relationships just to meet physical needs. They recognize more and more that these relationships must nurture them spiritually, also.

Letting go in what were previously committed, romantic and sexual relationships may take on different forms and different meanings. It means letting go of dimensions—physical, emotional, mental or spiritual, in part or in full, that couples have previously shared or hoped to share. It also means, when possible, transmuting the relationship into one that can still embrace some newly defined scope of mutuality in purpose, such as being amicable enough so that you may co-parent children, continue as co-workers, or be friends. Sometimes further purpose and life work together exists. Sometimes the work that you both shared together is now concluding and both need to move on. Sometimes letting go means no further contact with one another on the earthly plane.

Even if two people find that their paths are now separating and they must go in different directions they can still love one another spiritually. They can support the Soul's growth of one another as they let go of each other. By attuning to their inner wisdom they can be guided to release one another compassionately, sincerely invoking the Universe that each would go forth and achieve their greatest good. So often couples will curse and even condemn the very footsteps of a former partner. These actions only bind your energies, further hindering and hampering your own progress and footsteps towards happiness.

Every person in your life is there for a reason. It is important to recognize that your relationship with a mate has happened for a reason and has been an opportunity for you both to learn valuable Soul lessons. *Do not disrupt bonds until your have been in deep communion and consultation with Spirit, your Master Consciousness within, for guidance.*

My former husband and I are friends and we both know that we would go to the end of the earth to come to the aid of one another. We are now both remarried to other mates that we have found. We have a caring and amicable relationship, mutually co-parenting our children.

Giving God thanks for the relationships we have known is an important step. However, I had other things as yet to work through on my *inner healing work* before this revelation would come—on the way to finding my true Soulmate. Giving thanks to the Universe for my first marriage would come later.

NOTES

Chapter Six

Staying The Course
On The Way To
Finding Your Soulmate

Dear God,
    Why is it that I cannot get him [my
Soulmate] out of my consciousness? I
know I must keep my eyes on you Father.
Seek ye first the Kingdom of God and all
things will be added unto you. I want a
love in my life but this has not happened
so far. You know my need Father, better
than I do.
    I seek union with my Soulmate. But in
the meantime Lord, I seek to serve you
with an abundance of love in my heart
radiating out to all I come in contact with.
In keeping my focus here I can get lots of
practice in loving all those in my midst.
Love them to the fullest measure.
    I will be an expert on loving by the time
I meet my Soulmate! I can use my God
given talents in the meantime to be a good
mother, friend, sister, worker.

Paramahansa Yogananda in his book, <u>How You Can
Talk With God</u>, says, "Make your life more simple and
put your whole mind on God." [12]

STEP 25

Continuing In Service—
Serving In The World While
Deeply Desiring Soulmate Union

Despite a deep desire and yearning for finding your Soulmate, it is important to make a deep commitment to continue to serve in the Divine Plan with all your heart, mind, body and soul. In that Higher or Christ Consciousness, it is important to fully commune with Spirit, God, that your service is not based on what is given or taken away, but comes from your earnest and steadfast aspiration to truly be of service in the world.

This is communicated from that deep heartfelt place within you with *absolute sincerity and conviction.* God must know that after praying our earnest prayers for our Soulmate we fully let go of this desire to God, while never missing a beat in our service whether our desire is made manifest or not. There is no bargaining or making our service contingent upon what God does or does not do, gives or takes away.

In the face of this deep desire and yearning, you must have the attitude that, *no matter what, I will continue to serve God with all my heart, mind, body and soul.* I had an unswerving commitment and aspiration to serve God even if my desire for my Soulmate in this lifetime was never fulfilled.

It is important to communicate to Spirit that you would live your life joyfully and without interruption in your aspiration to serve even if your Soulmate never appeared in this lifetime. *In a perfectly ordered and divine Universe nothing is wasted. God is thrifty.*

With this awareness comes a growing recognition that all your prayers, meditations and earnest efforts move you closer to the lifetime in which you and your Soulmate will meet. Even if you do not meet your Soulmate in this lifetime no effort is wasted and each effort moves you closer to your Soulmate Union.

MEDITATION

No Matter What
I Will Continue To Serve

Reflect upon the previous passage,
allowing yourself to sit with the paradox of
desiring so deeply, yet letting go completely,
and putting your full attention
on your service in the world.

Communicate that you will continue to serve
in the Universe with all your heart, mind,
body and soul, with complete imperturbability
even if your desire to meet your Soulmate
in this lifetime is unfulfilled.

Say, "Thy Will be done. You, and You alone
know the perfect outworking and
timing of all things."

STEP 26

Recognizing Your Need
To Give and Receive Love

Dear God,
I have tremendous feelings of love
which I project toward this man, my
Soulmate. I think about him often.
I recognize it is not so much the man as
it is my need to find an object of affection
that can bear and be a vessel for my
feelings and reflect these back.

What would it be like for you to love someone and
have him or her love you back? The need to express love
is in us. We have love to give and we look for someone
who can contain or bear our love, as well as reflect that
love back to us.

Not only did I need to be loved, I had a tremendous
need to love someone in return. My heart ached as it
welled with love for a mate. The ache of welling was not
so different from the coinciding ache of emptiness and
longing that I also felt. The difference lay only in the
direction. Love needs to flow out from us and flow to us.

If we are blocked in receiving love we may feel empty,
and if we are blocked in expressing love we may feel welled
up in our hearts. Thus, we need to give and to receive
Love.

STEP 27

Making A Commitment To Life And Seeing All That Happens As Opportunities For Soul Growth

Dear God, Father, Mother of My Soul,
My need is so great. Where is my
Soulmate?
This test is the greatest. Yet what
benefit is it to test me when the tide is
out, when the welling is subsided?

I have come to see all life events, tests and challenges on my path as something to learn from. I give thanks to the Universe for the lessons these events teach me. I am eager to extract the essence of the lessons that each event on my path teaches. If I don't 'get it' or learn the lesson, I know it will be repeated in another form somewhere further down my path as I journey toward God.

As I experience each life challenge, I sit with the tension and a watchfulness of what may be revealed. I know my discomfort will be alleviated when revelation comes.

In 1980, I was on a retreat enjoying the silence when I had wonderful initiation into life experience. I was alone in a cottage on the Cape with my books and my journal. During this retreat experience I made the following journal entry:

Dear God, Father of My Soul,
Frequently on this journey, along this dusty road I had laid my baggage down, groveled in the dust, examined my blisters and sobbed in sorrow to God, asking, Why? Why go to the end of this journey and why the suffering along the way?

Now the questions have changed. I no longer ask, Why? I am not as concerned about what is at the end of the journey. I have picked up my load and the faith I have in taking that first step is the faith that sustains me each step of the way.

What sustains me is my love for you God, and your love for me. Suffering matters little. When I feel suffering, I remember that I believe, and I go on. It is as if suffering is only incidental to service. A bump along the way that I take little notice of, dwarfed and overshadowed as it is by the magnitude of the opportunity I feel.

The opportunity is in being a Co-worker and Co-creator in the Great Divine Plan to bring heaven to earth. I do not really suffer anymore. In fact, I'm done suffering. I know that in back of any felt sense of suffering is illumination. When illumination comes forth into consciousness then the challenge that had overshadowed will dissipate and fall away from my life.

I enjoy the expanse in consciousness that has been wrought by these lessons and I open to the next life lesson on my path. All provide me with opportunity for growth in this grand Univers(ity).

With recognition let me now walk this journey with joy, joy in service to the Most High.

James Allen writes the following: "Suffering is always the effect of wrong thought in some direction. It is an indication that the individual is out of harmony with himself, with the Law of his being. The sole and supreme use of suffering is to purify, to burn out all that is useless and impure. Suffering ceases for him who is pure ... a perfectly pure and enlightened being could not suffer." [13]

STEP 28

Focusing On Your
Greater Ache And Longing
For Union With God

Journal continued ...
I go on, I must go on and my ultimate goal must remain God. I cannot pursue and become lost in the dazzle of the trinkets along the way.
Focus on what you have, Terri, not on what is missing.
My greater ache is due to my increasing desire for knowledge of God and self.

Even though I sat with the ache of longing for my Soulmate, it gave me perspective to recognize my greater ache and longing was for union with God. This greater focus always predominated my awareness. I was continually seeking to deepen my conscious connection with God. He is my nearest, dearest, and eternally closest friend. Remember that no matter how much you desire this union with your Soulmate, *a Soulmate is just someone on the path as you make your way toward God.*

MEDITATION

Meeting And Re-meeting Your Soulmate On The Path Of Return To God

Reflect for a moment on the following:

A Soulmate is someone you meet
and re-meet along the way.
A Soulmate, like other life events,
holds the possibility for reawakening
and strengthening your union with God.

Do you reflect upon your divine goodness
daily? Who or what in your life is a daily
reminder to you of your divine goodness?

Imagine sharing your life with a mate
who reflects your divine goodness to you.
Now, imagine that you reflect the divine
goodness of your mate to him or her.

Imagine the spiritual validation both of you
will bring to each other's life.

STEP 29

Groveling, Marveling, Or Serving—
Beware And Keep Moving Forward

February 16, 1985

Dear God,
Help me to be right where I am and to accomplish the tasks that are specific to where I am. Help me to work in a spirit of joy, happiness and love and to inspire joy, happiness and love in those I meet along the way.

February 18, 1985

Dear God, Father, Mother of My Soul,
What is beyond the stresses of daily living, the recognition of what we have, the pining over what we do not have and the reviewing of the past?
What is beyond this? Oh Father, I wish I could see. Where can my mind light? What can it light upon?

It was not easy to desire my Soulmate so strongly, feel intense loneliness, and have a joyful countenance. I was doing some groveling at this point on my way to finding my Soulmate. I had three children. One was a teenager facing his own life challenges. As a psychotherapist I was working full time providing clinical services in an agency and in my private practice. I was going to be a single parent in just a few months. I was more attuned than ever to my emotional and cognitive dissonance. I could not reconcile in my heart and mind the question, *How could I have felt so excruciatingly lonely, all these years, while having been in a relationship with someone?*

Sometimes we grovel about life's conditions. To grovel means to lie flat or move with one's face to the ground. It is pining and agonizing, and grumbling over what is or is not. Sometimes we marvel about life's condition. To marvel means to lift our face with astonishment to the marvelous, the miraculous. You may marvel over something said, or done, or the way something or someone looks, for example. At times we can find ourselves groveling or marveling over what has happened in our life.

There is a time to mourn as well as a time to take note of the wondrous and miraculous. Each is important and necessary on the way to finding your Soulmate. But beware of excesses in either direction when it comes to groveling or marveling. Have you lost valuable time in groveling and pining? One can literally grovel and pine a lifetime away. On the other hand, one may feel it is better to lose time marveling. Perhaps. It is wonderful to marvel at some event in our lives or at some tremendously difficult step we were able to take and succeed at accomplishing. But this too may keep us focused upon what we did yesterday and we may lose valuable time. Imagine for example if Moses had stopped to marvel at what God had done through him in parting the Red Sea. Pharaoh's army would have gained ground. Surely the seas would have come crashing in again upon him and upon those he was sent to make a way for. He had to appreciate this miraculous accomplishment but also use it to move in a forward direction.

Have you known people who spend most of their time groveling or marveling about what happened in the past but who have not done much since? Receive your blessings like Moses and Go! Recognize your losses and go on! Attention to this step will aid you on your way to finding your Soulmate. Groveling and marveling can become distractions from service to the Divine plan and can keep you in the past. Start anew with what God has in store for you *in this moment.*

MEDITATION

Starting Anew In This Moment

Reflect for a moment on the times that you
have felt triumphs and defeats.
Recognize the power each has had to spur
you to move forward into greater service.

You should not feel stunned by the
miracles in your life, nor tarry great lengths of
time in the defeats from the past.
Give praise and appreciation for the special
fruit each renders, and move forward in
service. Neither groveling or marveling should
stop you in your tracks in service.

NOTES

Chapter Seven

Doing The Work Of Inner Healing

STEP 30

Managing Powerful Feelings

Journal continued ...
I am easy to distract. Remember I said that the only reason for going, the only aim was my love for you. You are the reason I take the first step and you are the reason for every step thereafter.
But alas, I am easy to distract ...

Often, it is hard to keep your mind on God. Keeping your mind attuned to the Divine will and purpose for your life can be very challenging. We can become so steeped in the demands of daily living that we are temporally hampered in our efforts to lift our hearts and minds to the abundance that awaits us. We become distracted by the mundane and unable to focus on the larger plan and purpose for our life.

Journal continued ...
Then what about my commitment and
promise that I have made to you? What
about my destiny? Help me oh Lord, to
keep my eyes, mind, heart, focused on the
goal. Depression has thrown me in the
past.

Sometimes powerful feelings about past events can grip your life, as they did mine. They can temporarily color our whole aura and seem to have a life of their own. I am a person of unshakable faith. Yet I, perhaps like yourself, had experienced certain impacts in life. These eventually caught up with me when I was in my late twenties, leading me to experience a dark night of the Soul on my spiritual journey. I recall how I experienced strong feelings of depression during that period of time. I had always known a deep communion with God from the time I opened my conscious eyes yet during that time period I could not seem to find God anywhere. At the time I wrote the following poem:

Depression

Depression is a friend of mine
It's the only thing I know
It locks me in its timeless grip
It follows me wherever I go
It cries with me to sleep each night
It wakes me up at dawn
It's the only thing that cared to stay
When faith and hope where gone.

Later I would realize that Spirit was working in a powerful way within me to transform my life. But at that time, even in my darkest hour, I sat quietly and prayed:

Dear God,
Guide me in Thy truth and instruct me
as you have done until now. Do not remain
silent. For thou art the God of my salva-
tion, you are the Light of my life. To Thee I
pray, for only you are worthy, on Thee I
wait all day.

When the darkness lifted, I was filled with a light such as never before experienced in its brilliance and illumination. Gone were the brittle and lifeless patterns that no longer contained my life, for these were stripped away. I was made new, my wholeness restored.

This transformation occurred as I sat within that broken place, knowing the old was shattered, and waiting to emerge into the new that had yet to unfold and reveal itself. In faith I held on.

How can you shed that which is brittle and lifeless from your own life? What powerful feelings have gripped you from the impacts, events, or challenges that you have experienced in your life? Is it fear, anger, anxiety, depression, resentment, victimization, and so on?

What is the powerful or favored feeling for you? Favored in the sense that your whole being has been dominated by its expression over all other feelings at some point in your life. Have you at some point favored this feeling over feelings such as joy, gratitude, or peace? For example, have you ever known someone who is always angry? Even when they could legitimately be sad or afraid they also convert these feelings into anger because that is what they know best and feel most familiar and comfortable. In my practice I have counseled many people who have over-used and even worn out a feeling by continuing to steep in it.

EXERCISE

What Favored Feeling Is
In Need Of Healing?

How do you feel?
Do you feel for example that self pity
is <u>a friend of yours</u>? Or, _____ is a
friend of mine. (Fill in the blank).
Then, ask yourself if you could
tolerate feeling something different.

People today are dealing with the past (and present) impacts of separations, psychological/sexual/physical abuses, addictions, losses, deaths, illness, and so on. These events stir strong feelings such as anger, sadness, guilt, violation, anxiety, and fear of abandonment. These feeling can color our life.

Strong feelings reflect your attempt to attune to, cope with and transform painful life events into the sweetness of illuminating insight. These feelings inform you of the work that needs to be done and allow you to hone in on the exact nature of that work. If you feel fear, ask yourself, What am I afraid of? If you feel anger ask yourself, What am I angry about? If it is guilt or shame you feel ask yourself, To what life event or events on my path are these feelings connected?

There is no missing the target if you allow your strong feelings to guide you right to the core issue that demands your attention and demands that you work it through. By working through a problem rather than avoiding or anesthetizing our feelings we are spiritually expanded. We grow larger rather than smaller. Dr. Scott Peck writes that working through the legitimate suffering that results from life's problems allows us to be expanded spiritually whereas avoiding the problem and its attendant pain leads to a shriveling of the Spirit. [14]

You probably know someone who experienced a painful event and coped with this event through life negating behavior, avoiding, or anesthetizing themselves. You may see that these choices led to the shriveling of their spirit and how they have not been able, up to this point, to grow past this event.

STEP 31

Working Through
Painful Life Events

The only way out is through. We grow spiritually by working through the challenges that life presents to us and not by moving to the right or to the left, leaping over, tunneling underneath, dulling our awareness with drugs, or by attempting to disappear our problems. How else will we extract the spiritual essence of these challenges unless we sit with them and intimately embrace them? We must face and work through the challenges that present on our journey. I know that this work can be very difficult, and that it takes a lot of courage.

On the way to finding your Soulmate strong feelings may surface about the impacts you have experienced in your life from past events and the wounds and pain these have caused you. As you go through the process of invoking the Universe for your Soulmate other strong feelings such as your worthiness to even ask for this event in your life (and described later in this book) may also surface. In both instances these feelings need to be managed and worked through.

Whatever strong feelings, memories or events shade your life you can begin right where you are now to transform your situation by strengthening your connection with the Divine Presence within you. There is no time like the present to just begin. These feelings are helpful pointers to the exact nature of the work that needs to be done to restore you to a sense of wholeness. That they are surfacing now is an indicator of your readiness and preparedness to deal with them.

Let your inner wisdom guide you to find the answers and the supports along the way that you will need. Commit yourself to the *process* of working through these feelings and events.

During the process of invoking your Soulmate, your Divine connection will give you what you need to work through whatever strong feelings may arise so that you are not thrown by these in achieving your good and manifesting your goal.

MEDITATION

Trusting The Universe
For Needed Healing

I am in complete trust that the Universe
will provide me with all that is needed
to work through my emotional pain
and to be restored to wholeness.
I extract the spiritual essence that these
lessons have taught me and I garner the fruit.

I draw upon the Infinite Fount of all greatness
and goodness for my supply. (Repeat 3 times.)

I attract those people and situations into my
life that will facilitate my healing and aid my
illumination. I know my complete healing is
assured. I am done feeling _____
(fill in the blank: badly, fearful, angry,
sickly, guilty, ashamed, etc.)

I am done suffering. (Repeat 3 times).

I now open to experience feelings I have
not felt very often, like, joy, peace of mind,
bliss and unconditional love.
I know these feelings may not be as familiar
to me as these others, but I open to being
able to bear and tolerate this change
as these feelings begin to
predominate my daily experience.
I know that in moving to these newly
experienced states of being that a change

in my spiritual vibration is occurring
and I welcome this change. I open to
a higher spiritual vibration.

My instrument easily and graciously
opens and adapts to this new vibration.
(Repeat 3 times.)

STEP 32

Opening The Doorway
To Abundance

Just how long do you think it takes for you to right
yourself in relationship to the Universe so that you are
aligned with the Infinite Fount of abundant good and
blessings?

Sometimes when I would open to the Universe to receive the abundance I knew awaited me, almost immediately this would be followed by a replaying of past events
in my life which I felt badly about. In those moments I
would experience a welling up of guilt, shame or unworthiness. Then suddenly, I would feel the aperture or opening through which Universal goodness flows through me
automatically snap shut—thus cutting me off from this
wellspring of joy, abundance, and all participation in
greater life.

STEP 33

Removing The Blockages

When we start to align ourselves within the *stream of abundance* so that good things are either starting to come our way or are happening now, we often start to worry that something will go wrong. We can wonder if we deserve the goodness that is flowing into our lives. I see this happening often in the lives of people I work with in therapy. As they begin to move in this stream where things are going well for them they often quickly find themselves feeling misconnected once again from their Divine source. This is due to a return of thoughts, feelings or actions which set them back into that old sense of dis-ease, closing them off again to conditions of prosperity. I will often ask clients, "Couldn't you stand to feel so good and to have things going so well?" The answer is usually a qualified, "No."

The vibration of the *good* that we envision for ourselves does not match the vibration of the *negative or bad* feelings we experience on the inside. This is one reason why we close off in that moment. We find ourselves unable to tolerate the disparity that these two distinct types of feelings bring.

These feelings carry differing qualities of energy and vibrations. We must learn to bear the vibration of good feelings. For example, just as we learn how to bear the vibration of anger we need to learn to bear the vibration of pride. Did anyone ever give you a surprise party, a compliment, or some recognition in which you felt so much pride you thought you would topple over? In that moment you had to bear or tolerate the vibratory quality of pride. Similarly we must learn to bear happiness, joy and abundance.

It is also part of our Divine inheritance to experience bliss. Bliss is an inner joy unconnected to any external happening and arises out of a deep and profound internal state of being. In other words, this feeling does not rise or fall with the changes in your outer circumstance. It flows from the realization of your Oneness with Spirit, God.

MEDITATION

**The Experience
Of Inner Joy (Bliss)**

Please ponder the following questions:

Would you recognize a feeling of
inner joy or bliss if you experienced it?
Could you bear its vibration?
Would you need to label it something
else or reject it all together?

Can you seek and find a blissful
union with someone else
before you have experienced,
and are able to bear,
this bliss within you?

STEP 34

Forgiving

On the way to finding your Soulmate you must believe that you deserve the event of having a loving relationship. You must give yourself permission to open fully to this experience and you must be able to bear the high vibratory quality of this energy.

We need to first explore how we have gotten in our own way, thus blocking the abundant Universal flow to us. Opening to this experience means having the willingness and the courage to remove any and all blocks that may hamper and impede the flow of good to you. Self forgiveness and forgiving others can be one of these major blocks.

It is important that you be willing to enter into a forgiveness process so that you may forgive whomever and whatever needs to be forgiven and to be open to receive forgiveness from whomever and whatever situations in your life.

EXERCISE

**Writing Down What
Needs Forgiving**

When you think about forgiveness,
ask yourself, Who or what needs
forgiving, or releasing?

Write down your responses
on a piece of paper. This list will
comprise your forgiveness work—and
it is just that—work.
You will want to commit yourself
to doing this work.

I thought I had mostly cleared up unfinished business with Spirit as regarded releasing events from the past and experiencing the forgiving, redeeming, and healing power of God. I was wrong. At times, I found that the very act of asking the Universe for the Soulmate I so desired stirred my fear and doubt, and raised questions within me as to whether I was worthy to receive this blessing or any blessing for that matter.

Memories from the past of times I felt I had fallen short would pounce upon my chest like a lion pouncing upon its prey, leaving me to feel heavy and bogged down. For a brief moment I even saw *the Universe* as *holding*

something against me and withholding from me as I began doubting whether or not I had been *fully forgiven*. I
thought, even if all the "little stuff" had been forgiven or
released, what about the "big stuff"?

I realized that I did have some unfinished business or
work—Forgiveness Work. I knew at that point in my life
that *I needed to fully realize God's forgiveness of me and
my forgiveness of myself.*

> **Dear God,**
> **I sought God's forgiveness and He
> responded ...**

Spirit revealed to me that if one accepts forgiveness
then one is healed. Healing follows forgiveness like night
follows day. But how long does forgiveness take? How
long does it take you, for example, to forgive yourself or
someone else? A week, a month, a year? Do you also
believe that God needs *TIME* to forgive? I came to learn
in the words of Ruby Dee [15] that *God's forgiveness is
instantaneous.*

> **Dear God,**
> **You say, "You are forgiven, now go
> forward." I charge that you have not
> forgiven me. So, I fear and regress. What a
> lot of nerve I have to doubt you in this way
> Father!**
> **How can I be faithful and a server when
> you say, "You are forgiven," and I lay in
> fear that what you say is not so? Oh
> doubter that I am and what faith do I
> have in the asking if I doubt the outcome?**

There is an intimate connection between *forgiveness and healing.* If one feels worthy of forgiveness then one is healed. On the way to accepting the gift of a Soulmate I needed to accept God's forgiveness totally so that I could then be healed of and release all the things of the past. *If God's forgiveness is instantaneous, but I could not accept this event in my consciousness until the passage of some time period, then the manifestation of my healing would also be delayed by this same time period.*

I realized that God had long ago bestowed this blessing of Instantaneous Forgiveness to me even though I was not fully ready to receive it, nor felt worthy—until now. As I now accepted this blessing God's healing became *real* in my life and doubt and fear vanished.

But even after working through this step I next needed to forgive myself which I realized took a lot longer. I found that feeling some up or elation about the prospect of being in a loving relationship can be followed by a down. What makes being, or the prospect of being, in a committed relationship so wonderfully self revealing in its power is that the very heat of this love crucible causes all that is impure and needs to be worked on to rise to the surface. This purificatory fire is one of the special gifts given by Spirit to those undergoing preparation to meet their Soulmate.

I realized that I was much quicker at forgiving others than I was at forgiving myself. I needed to learn how to more approximate the Spirit of instantaneously forgiving myself, rather than delaying the manifestation of this event in my consciousness for days, months, or even years. I needed to learn to imitate God more in the Spirit of instantaneous forgiveness or release when it came to myself. Even if I could not be totally instantaneous like God, I could at least approximate this by shortening the interval between an event in which I felt I had erred and the event of my forgiving my human self. With this illumination from Spirit I was now more fully able to release myself from the past and open to the future without as many impediments or blockages to the bountifulness of the Universe. The ability to be able to forgive oneself (and others) becomes a tool which sweeps the path continually—clearing any blockages to the gifts of Spirit. We need to be able to stand when our Father God says, Where are you Adam, Where are you Eve. We need to stand unbowed and confident answering, Here I am. Having a forgiveness process operating in our lives allows us to stand.

> **Dear God,**
> **I now move forward, onward, fearless**
> **and confident in you, God, Father, Mother**
> **of my Soul.**

AFFIRMATION

Claiming Forgiveness

In entering a forgiveness process,
say the following:

If I am forgiven by God then I am healed.
I accept that I have been
totally forgiven by God.
I am forgiven by God therefore I am healed.
I love and forgive myself totally
and I am healed.
I shorten the interval of time it takes
to forgive myself.

If God's forgiveness of me is instantaneous
then I move to approximate more of
God's love and grace by forgiving and
releasing myself and others from the past.

All the clouds that have blurred
this reality are now lifted.
I now claim my Divine inheritance of
a joyful and loving relationship.

Any and all blockages to the abundant
flow of Divine blessings are removed.
My forgiveness is a given,
therefore, healing must follow.
When one manifests, so does the other.

As we try to cross that threshold to greater abundance all the doubts and feelings of unworthiness can surface. These have to be mastered before you can truly enter into this greater abundance.

You may feel dejected. As you recall the things that make you feel unworthy you may sigh, Oh what's the use? You might ask, How will I surmount this mountain of stuff that acts as an obstacle to the receipt of my good and Divine inheritance? You may feel out of touch with your Master Consciousness or that God has not been a strong presence in your life or has abandoned you in the past. Sometimes you might demandingly ask to know, How come I had to go through this or that experience in the first place? Then there may be moments when you cry from the depths of your Soul, Oh God, Why did I have to experience this pain and loss of innocence along the way? I know I and many of the people I have worked with have asked some or all of these questions.

Dear Father, Mother, God,
    As regards my healing I ask at this
time, "Why did I have to stray so far?" To
which you reply,
    So I could show my love for you to the
nth degree."

There is no distance we can stray that Divine and Infinite Love cannot embrace us. God's grace is with us. If we but ask.

The inability to forgive and release others for the impacts that they have had on your life can be another block in receiving your good. Even though it can be extremely difficult somehow we must come to see everyone who comes into our life and their actions as there to cultivate our strengths and spiritual gifts, particularly the gift of love. Again, sometimes the persons or events that need forgiving represent major traumas in one's life and often require a lot of supportive skill and counsel in this healing process.

Hurts caused by others in the present moment can stir up memories of hurts caused by others in the past. Hurts are linked together like the cabs of a train—pull one and they all come along—as reverberations from earlier hurts are drawn into the present moment. Hurts from the past can also stir up fears about future hurts and losses. You can find yourself not only reacting to the present hurt, anger, slight or loss, but summing those that have occurred from the past and bringing them into the present moment. Instead of directing 100 ohms of anger, hurt, frustration, anxiety and so on at the person or situation in the present moment which would be appropriate you may unleash a 500,000 volt response instead.

Due to the strong link between past, present and even future hurts forgiving big hurts especially ones that have come early in life can remove old as well as newer blockages in your energy flow. *Forgiveness keeps you an open channel ready to receive from an abundant Universe.*

Often, as part of your healing, you are called to love and forgive that very person whom you find undeserving and unlovable. When you forgive and love someone who is undeserving and has done nothing to earn your love and forgiveness then you are expressing unconditional love.

Those who are undeserving and unlovable test you to cultivate the consciousness of loving unconditionally and universally. Give thanks and appreciation to that person who has been so unkind to you. Thank them for their willingness to suffer in being the awful person that they have been so that they could teach and give you the gift of unconditional and universal love. There is something in it for you when you are moved to love and forgive in this way. This is often alluded to when a client has said, "Well if I can love and forgive him (or her) for what he has done to me, then I can love and forgive anyone." There is a profound truth in these words.

Sometimes people are in need of forgiving God. They will report, "I am mad at God, how could he have let this happen to me? God is not there for me. I have no God." One can scarcely imagine what a difficult situation this must be for the Universe when we turn our back on it in supposition that it has turned its back on us first.

Look up at the night sky in search of your reconnection. Pray. Take long walks in nature, taking time to note God's presence everywhere. Remember, your connection is always present even when memory, belief, or faith in this connection temporarily fail you.

STEP 35

Making A Place Within You
For This Sacred Union

Dear God,
You are first and last, Dear God. Help
me to be joyful and to continually be in
that state of joyfulness. Help me to go on
and serve you.
Fill this ache, this void or help me to
erase it from my consciousness.
How can I go around with this crater?
What will occupy my mind?

Strongly desiring Soulmate union also means making a place within your being to receive your Soulmate. Creating a place for your Soulmate means you are open and receptive to receive this event. This requires holding a certain tension in your being.

This is the tension of expansiveness, especially when you would just as easily snap shut, close off, and not experience the vulnerability of a call as yet unanswered, a request as yet unfulfilled.

Be willing to sit with the ache of it, sometimes experienced as a void or emptiness inside. That gaping hole feeling inside you is waiting to be filled by the one you love. As much as I tried to raise my consciousness completely above this feeling and its attendant pain, at times, I could not. Allow me to clarify here that I did not feel like a completely empty vessel waiting to be filled. My life

was very full. I had a wonderful family, friends, and service in the world that I loved. Yet, something was missing. What I mean by "empty" is that I did not feel fulfilled
in having a relationship with a mate who I could love
spiritually, mentally, emotionally, and physically and be
loved by, in these ways, in return.

You may find that your life is so filled with career,
friends, travel, and other interests that you not only feel
fulfilled, but you could not possibly make room in your
life for the event of a Soulmate or perhaps any seriously
committed romantic relationship. Many people today, for
example, struggle with whether to make a place in their
lives to receive a child. Similarly, being in a loving committed relationship requires that one go through the steps
of strongly desiring this event and making room to grate-
fully, lovingly, and joyously receive fully this event into
their life.

I feel that sitting with the ache of it is necessary preparation for receiving. However, in retrospect, I now see
that if I possessed at that time even more of a spirit of
"gratitude" and "have" as described by Price [16] that more
of my discomfort would have been eased on the way to
finding my Soulmate. This means having even more of
an attitude of thankfulness even though my Soulmate
still remained invisible, and acting as if I already "have"
what I have asked the Universe for. This may be hard to
do yet I share this with you in the hope that it will help
you to better bear the tension of receptivity, openness,
and awaiting.

Say the following Affirmations as a demonstration of
being grateful for what has already been granted to you
even though it still remains invisible:

AFFIRMATION

Giving Thanks For Your Mate
Before He Or She Appears

Thank you God for creating
that perfect mate for me.

I openly receive this loving relationship.

The beautiful intertwining
of our lives
is unfolding.

Your perfect mate exists for you. Give abundant praise to Spirit for the knowingness that he or she is real and exists, even if he or she has not yet precipitated out on the physical plane so that you can behold him or her in this lifetime with your physical eyes.

You always have an inner plane or subjective connection with your Soulmate.

STEP 36

Finding Strength And Comfort
In Divine Spirit

March 12, 1985

Dear God, Father, Mother, Of My Soul,
Thank you for my peace of mind and
the stillness and calmness of heart.
Thank you for the evenness and balance I
feel and my sense of completeness and
wholeness.
I am learning to be loving and kind in
the face of adversity. My preparation
continues. I continue to develop the ability
to serve. I love myself and I am centered
within. I know who I am and where I
dwell. These are wonderful gifts.

March 24, 1985

Dear God,
What lessons have I learned in these
last few difficult months?
I have learned that you are with me
always. You are with me when others
doubt me. You are with me when a thou-
sand eyes search my being, scanning me
for imperfections or a place to attack.
You are with me when there are clouds
overhead. You are with me when the sun
is shining brightly.

*What does it matter that the world
around me is changing? Our togetherness
is eternal. Only my relationship with you
is a constant. It is a constant source of
comfort, love, warmth, and tenderness. It
is a constant source of caring, support,
understanding and forgiveness. You are
my nearest and dearest friend. You are my
comforter. These external events only test
my knowledge of you and my faith in you.
You are the Light of my life. Let me do
what is pleasing to you God.*

*I am sustained. I have called on Thee
from the cradle. I have searched for Thee
from the time I opened my conscious eyes
and could see.*

July 29, 1985

Dear God,
*On you I depend, in you I put my faith.
Jay left tonight. This is my first night
alone. I cried but feel inner peace at my
center. God gives and he takes away. Your
grace is sufficient unto me.*

There was a special feeling that arose inside of me on
that night. Whatever the cosmic drama was that Jay and
I had together, it had run its course and come to an end.

We were now released to go on with our lives. I was
neither angry nor bitter. I was just done! I felt a sense of
relief. I knew my work with Jay as a mate was com-
pleted; there was no more for the two of us to do together. We had long begun the work of transforming our
relationship from one that had been previously romantic and sexual to one in which we could be friends or at

least friendly enough so that we could co-parent our children. I had taken the responsibility for initiating this change in my life. I was now a single parent with three children. I opened to the unknown future, but a future I felt would be responsive to my needs.

August 4, 1985

Dear God of My Soul,
   I bid my heart not to fear nor to pine.
Divine Love always has met, always will
meet every human need.

I had faith that my every need would be met by Spirit. I had faith in a brighter future. I let go and let God.

Journal Continued ...
   Let it not be said that all you have to
do to make Terri cease seeking and serv-
ing God is take away her mate and give
her a lonely night! You are the Light of my
life, to Thee I pray. You are my salvation,
on Thee I wait all day.

EXERCISE

**What Could Interrupt
Your Seeking And Serving?**

Answer the following question for yourself.

What would it take for you to
stop seeking and serving your Higher Power?

All you have to do to make me stop seeking
and serving God is_____(fill in).

Again it is important to maintain an unswerving commitment to be of service in the world, even when you feel
emotionally burdened.

STEP 37

Enhancing Your Self Esteem
Hastens Your Soulmate Union

August 13, 1985

Dear God,
I feel I am this beautiful, loving, warm, tender, gentle and sensitive human being with no one to love me spiritually, mentally, emotionally and physically.
I cry and yearn and sometimes fear but I go on.

Yes, I said beautiful—along with other wonderful qualities. I did not always feel I was beautiful. I had to evolve to a felt sense of inner and outer beauty. It is important to affirm your qualities. If you think you are ugly, fat, bald, stupid, insensitive, unlovable and boring then there is more work to be done on your self esteem. The quest for your Soulmate is an inner one. Do the inner work to raise your spiritual vibration to hasten this union.

By invoking the Universe for your Soulmate you are asking to love another and to be loved in return. Love is one of the most powerful forces in the Universe. *Love will stir up all of your stuff. All your feelings of self doubt, lack, or unworthiness.*

When you think about and actually meet your Soulmate it will stir you to ask yourself questions like, What will he or she think or feel about this or that aspect of my life or of who I am? Allow these thoughts and feelings to come up as you are steeped in thoughts of your Soulmate. Resolve how you feel as each issue surfaces. This will aid you in doing the work of self healing—allowing you to stand more confidently in your sense of wholeness and self acceptance.

Love is the great purifier, like burning the dross from gold, love causes all that is impure to rise to the surface to be siphoned off, leaving pure gold. Poor self esteem has to be worked through in order to increase your capacity to love more and to be loved more fully in return.

Be willing to enter into this purification process. In many ways maintaining low self esteem is a selfish act because it inhibits you from giving fully to a mate (and to others). There are a multiplicity of opportunities today to engage in experiences that raise your self esteem. There are groups, workshops, self help workbooks, and therapies. All of these can aid your spiritual, psychological, emotional and physical development. Take responsibility for your healing and listen to your inner wisdom for guidance along the way.

As previously mentioned, you may notice that when you think about good things happening, or when something good does happen in your life, it may raise questions in you about whether you are deserving of these events. *Not feeling good about yourself can make you snap shut against this flow of good from the Universe, thus closing you off to these experiences.* Actually it is this good that is attempting to flow to you that you may feel you must ward off so that strong feelings about being deserving do not become triggered. This pattern can keep you from working through important life issues thus keeping you from receiving abundantly from the Universe.

I have known people who have interacted coarsely with others to ward off loving displays by others. These individuals did not feel they deserved to be loved or shown any kindness. Somehow they came to believe that it was easier to interact with the world in this way rather than to work through the painful issues that made them feel so nondeserving in the first place.

As we journey through life our brilliant Soul Light may become caked and crusted by the mud, illusion (Maya) or impacts of daily living. The beautiful Soul qualities we each possess may be temporarily obscured. We recover by uncovering the Soul, its tremendous light, love, wisdom and power. We must unearth our Soul Light so that it shines brightly and clearly out into the world. We must unveil the many layers of distortion we have about who we are and fully embrace our Higher Self by standing in this Soul Light.

There is a cartoon caption that shows a huge auditorium with row after row of seats. In the back of the auditorium is a huge banner that reads, 'Adult Children of Normal Families.' There are only two people in the audience! This tells the story all too well that many people are in Recovery from families and other relationships.

Many of us have the experience of coming from families or other relationships where we did not feel valued or loved. The dynamics of having others relate to you in a negative way turns into the baggage that you can carry and use to replicate these same dynamics in future relationships. In other words, if you have had the experience of being treated in a way that fosters low self esteem you may recreate situations in current relationships that mirror back to you what feels familiar. This is a condition that begs attention and healing. Do the work of Self restoration. You deserve to experience fully your wholeness and goodness.

Painful life events occur that erode self esteem and it is important to make every effort to recover and restore the Soul. Some people have experienced events which they, seemingly, will not recover from in their entire lifetime. These events bind them, lock them in a time warp and rob them from fully expressing the joy of the Soul.

On the one hand, I am comforted in the knowledge that the Soul will have its way and will fully express itself no matter how many lifetimes it takes. On the other hand, I strongly support having *a rapid recovery time by healing in this lifetime.* Do everything in your power to hasten your healing and transformation.

In using a psycho-spiritual approach to therapy, I supports individuals to shorten the interval between a painful, traumatic, self esteem eroding life event and one's actual recovery from that event. This, of course, does not mean that we ever forget the event. What it does mean is that we extract the spiritual food from these painful experiences, thereby experiencing an expansion of the Soul, and we go on.

AFFIRMATION

Healing In This Lifetime

I will work to heal in this lifetime.
I will shorten the interval of time
between a painful event in my life
and my recovery from that event.

I extract the spiritual food from
life's experiences. These experiences provide
the spiritual food that my Soul
needs to grow and evolve.

I am a loving being, worthy to receive
Divine blessings. I open my heart and mind.
I pour forth love to others.

I open to the abundance of the Universe and
receive my good. I generously give and receive.
I release any and all blockages
to the flow of this good.

I am a perfect child of God.
I reclaim my wholeness and divinity.
I open to a loving relationship
with my Soulmate.

STEP 38

**Holding Onto Your Ideal,
Your Vision For A Soulmate Union**

August 15, 1985

Dear God,
*I must be willing and I am willing to
give up that one thing that I now desire
most on earth, a loving relationship with
my Soulmate. It has not come to pass and
I want to move on with my life. I hate the
feeling of feeling stuck. I will concentrate
on my work. So much time wasted already. Thy will be done.*

August 25, 1985

Dear God, Father of My Soul,
   It seems that tears and weekends go together. I cannot give up my ideal, my Soulmate. I desire so much to meet him, to be with him, to share my life and my love with him.

I think it is natural for doubt to surface. As well as the going back and forth over whether to stay open to the experience of finding your Soulmate. Even if the object of your ideal does not appear during your lifetime you do not have to give up your *IDEAL.* Nor do you suddenly lose your ideal. The archetype of your perfect, loving union is within you.

I work with many men and women in psychotherapy who have experienced a breakup in a relationship, or who are trying to find a mate. I tell them that just because the object of their love has gone, or has not been located, they do not have to let go of their ideal. Often they feel that with the breakup of a relationship they also lose their vision of a future happiness lived and shared with a mate—harmoniously suited for them. Suddenly their vision of being wed, sharing a long life with a mate and having a family is all lost.

The vision that you have spun with the golden threads of your higher aspiration is not lost even if the one who would fulfill that vision has not yet appeared. Do not let go of your vision!

Love is inside you. You will find the mate who will reflect back that love. Hold onto your ideal and vision of a divinely loving union on earth in spite of your history in male/female relationships and in the face of any evidence to the contrary.

Dear God,
*   He is not just anyone, he is the only*
one, my Soulmate. Bring us together
Father, join us in our sacred union as you
have joined us in lifetimes past.

STEP 39

Dealing With Doubts
And Probabilities

You may ask, What are the chances of finding my Soulmate? I know as an African American women familiar with so-called data on male/female ratios, I admit that I wondered what the statistical probability was of finding any mate, let alone a Soulmate.

Yet, I remembered what my mother would always say to me especially when I would say something could not be accomplished, for this or that reason. She would ask, "What does that have to do with you?" She would say that this or that reason, circumstance or hindrance had nothing to do with me and I was encouraged to move through whatever the perceived obstacle might be.

During my early years, naturally, I felt this or that hindrance did have something to do with me, and I would walk away feeling her statement had disqualified my feelings and concerns. However I have come to value this perspective because it has pushed me to expand my thinking about many things. *After all, we must ask ourselves the question, Who or what can rob me of my natural divine inheritance, the fruits of an abundant and giving universe?*

You must believe deep in your heart that you will find your Soulmate. Any so called evidence to the contrary must be met with your affirming, "What does that have to do with me?" If you have prayed your earnest prayer, turn it over to God. Then with earnest and steadfast aspiration to serve, play your part fully as a coworker in the Divine Plan, with the conviction that your service is not based upon what God gives, does not give or takes away. *Affirm, Thy Will Be Done.* Then you are on your way to finding your Soulmate.

Again, remember that if this event does not occur in this lifetime that in a Divinely ordered Universe, nothing is ever wasted. Your efforts, prayers, faith, and service pass with you from one portal of life to the next moving you closer to the lifetime in which you and your Soulmate will be united on the physical/earthly plane.

STEP 40

Being Joyful About
Just Being And Becoming

When I prayed and meditated, I did so with a heart filled with love and faith in God. Each word spoken was imbued with love and faith. I felt very blessed in my life and I had absolute faith in Divine guidance. I was filled with a joy and happiness about life. I smiled often. A smile, not due to any particular external reason or event but out of a joy inside. It is not that I found a million dollars. It is learning to smile your inner secret and sacred smile. It is smiling on the inside. It is a joyfulness about just being and becoming.

Dear God, Father, Mother of My Soul,
*　　I may learn to go on but I cannot, will*
not give up my ideal, I pray that you make
manifest my ideal.
*　　I pray that you manifest my Soulmate*
on the physical plane so that we may be
united soon.

I prayed and meditated continually for this union. I spoke to Spirit silently, audibly and through writing in my journal. In meditation and through my daily activities I listened for the voice of Spirit, that Still Small Voice inside.

Dear God,
*　　It is the longing and desire to find, to*
be with, to love and be loved by my
Soulmate that is not satiated or quenched
by anything else.

For me the desire was a burning ache. There could be no substitute.

Again, in desiring your Soulmate it is important that this desire be very strong. There are so many negative and heavy thought forms that surround relationships between men and women today. These are thoughts infused with anger, mistrust, and fear which interfere with the deeply loving and spiritual connection that can be sensed and known between mates. If you desire this blissful union then your desire must be strong enough to cut through the heavy thought forms which veil relationships on the planet today. *By holding onto your ideal you infuse the ethers with your remembrance of this divine union from the misty past.*

AFFIRMATION

Holding Onto Your Ideal

I hold onto my envisioned ideal of
a union harmoniously lived and
shared with my Soulmate.

STEP 41

Appreciating, Giving Thanks,
And Understanding Relationships
As Opportunities For Soul Development

August 27, 1985

Dear God, Father, of My Soul,
*   It dawns on me that I have not thanked*
you for my relationship with Jay. Despite
many things of which you are aware he
has aided my growth and development
tremendously and I pray I have aided him.
Many times he has been a friend, gener-
ous, and caring.

We have produced beautiful children out of this union and I did grow to love him. Thank you for what Jay and I have shared.

There is much to be said about all the opportunities every relationship brings. I see relationships with people as *sacred encounters* in that each one offers an opportunity in time and space to do some work together, to love, to care, to share, to learn, to grow, and to expand the Soul's expression in its journey.

We may expect some relationships to last a lifetime, like with family. For example, I expect to share in a relationship with my mother as long as we may both live. Yet other relationships are of shorter duration. For example, I have never seen my kindergarten teacher again. Yet that was an encounter, nine months in duration, in which we came together, expressed caring, shared a work in common and then moved out of one another's life space. There are encounters with complete strangers that are just minutes in duration but have an impact on us. Everything and everyone teaches. People are our gurus in that every encounter teaches us something about ourselves.

As we journey through life we will find ourselves in relationship with others that we are romantically attracted to. Some of theses relationships are of short duration, some result in a long term commitment or marriage. Whatever romantic relationship you find yourself in, recognize that each offers the opportunity for your personal growth and development. Each provides an opportunity for you to discover who you are as you see and learn about the self. As we awaken to the soulfulness of ourselves we desire to have a soulful contact in another. A Soulmate is at first someone with whom we have a spiritual connection.

The question arises, What are you looking for in a relationship? Sometimes people are looking for someone who they are comfortable and compatible with physically and sexually. Sometimes people look for emotional companionship and seek relationship with one who can empathize with their feelings and be supportive of their emotional needs. Some are in search of mental mates— those who share compatible intellects and ideologies. When you are trying to find your Soulmate you look for one human being with whom you can cultivate all of these connections. It is wonderful to connect so fully with another in all of these ways!

Moreover, there is so much opportunity to learn about the self in committed male/female relationships. There is no accident when two people come together in time and space to share experiences. Your mate, even if this is not a Soulmate, teaches you much and reflects much to you about who you are. For example, our mates can teach us patience by reflecting back to us those times when we have been impatient. They may teach us compassion, strength, self love and many other wonderful qualities.

Often couples decide to part, not because they want less but because they have learned to seek *more* from a relationship. Parts of them have been awakened in the current relationship that now cry out for further expression, nurturance and development. To this expansion of awareness of who we are becoming we can give thanks, praise and appreciation to our mates, even if these are non Soulmate unions and these lessons have come with some amount of pain. Even an abusive relationship has the power to spur our indignation, awaken our self love and lead us to take new actions in our lives.

So often when there is a parting in male/female relationships there is a focus on how one or the other partner feels *diminished* rather than on how one has been *enhanced* by the union. Our mates may fulfill early unmet needs for security or companionship for example, which then allows us to awaken to other needs that we were less aware of until these earlier needs were met. That your mate is unable or unwilling to meet needs that arise later in the relationship does not discount the tremendous aid they have been to you in your journey. Often your mate will remind you of how he or she fulfilled some particular need you had or helped and supported you to develop some needed quality.

EXERCISE

Remembering The Gifts
Of Your Relationship(s)

Take time now to recognize
the many ways that your mate(s)
is (are) helping, or has helped,
you to learn valuable life lessons,
cultivate your strengths, and
express your spiritual gifts—all enabling
you to see and know yourself better.

Bring your awareness to the many ways
in which your life has been enhanced
by this (these) relationship(s).

I know that the things that happened in my first marriage enhanced and aided my Soul's growth and development. Both the pleasant and the unpleasant experiences contributed. I learned valuable lessons that prepared me for union with my Soulmate, lessons I could not have otherwise mastered. My first husband Jay loved me in his own way. In the beginning of our relationship I valued and trusted in that love, but when I learned to love myself more and more fully his way of loving me no longer felt good. He probably did not change the way he loved me. What changed was the way I loved myself.

The fact of the matter is that, when I changed the way I loved me I could no longer accept his way of loving me. I experienced an unfoldment in myself that then led me to want even more from my union with another. My higher centers were opened and stimulated from the joys and the pains of being in a long-term, committed relationship with Jay.

I would not have changed a thing on my way to finding my Soulmate because everything that happened along the way contributed to the successive preparation of my Soul for this union.

AFFIRMATION

**Giving Appreciation For
Your Relationship(s)**

I give thanks and appreciation for the
union that I have shared with
_____(fill in his/her name).

I give thanks for the experience wrought by
the life lessons we have undergone together.

You have enabled me to see the many
qualities within myself and also those
qualities I needed to develop more in this
lifetime and perhaps in the lifetimes to come.

I have learned more about what is
needed for my Soul's unfoldment,
both by what was present and by what
was missing in our relationship.

All that you have reflected to me
and all that has remained unreflected
has offered me the potential to see
what was needed within me more fully.
I pray that I have aided
your Soul awakening also.

May all good things come your way
as you continue in your journey.
May all that comes to both of us
as we now go our separate ways on the
physical plane draw us closer to
the Boundless All from which we both arose.

We will all be united
when we return to our source.
Our return comes when we experience a full
realization of our God Self.

NOTES

NOTES

Chapter Eight

Understanding Energy
And Soulmate Unions

As a little girl, I would sense the energy radiating from others around me. I noted for example how some people radiated a warmth, while others felt cold and detached. Others I knew to be wise or old souls and still others felt crafty and unpredictable. Some were very enthusiastic about life and others you had to be very, very neat and orderly around. I felt the energy radiated by others so keenly throughout my being that sometimes my very fingertips would tingle from all the stimulation of these energies.

Later, life would teach me to cover up and spiritually protect myself as I moved through the sea of energy that is all around us. Life would also teach me how to more accurately discern the various qualities of energy being radiated by another and to distinguish this energy from my own. I would observe and learn much from watching the interplay of these energies between myself and another. I would also observe and learn much from the interplay of energies between people, and groups.

STEP 42

Understanding The Qualities Of Energy
To Look For In A Mate

You too know much about energy. You might ponder for a moment and ask yourself what is it that you do sense or read about another when you say, for example, that they are warm, forceful, creative, or manipulative. You are sensing a particular quality of energy being radiated by that person.

Energy can be understood in terms of frequency and vibration. Each frequency and vibration produces a particular quality of energy. *It is these qualities that you are interested in attuning to and understanding on the way to finding your Soulmate.* By understanding these qualities you access valuable information and insight about your own energy makeup and the energy makeup you desire in a mate. Recognition of your Soulmate becomes possible through understanding energy.

You speak about qualities of energy when you talk about how you feel *good vibes versus bad vibes* in your encounter with another person. Energy is all around us. Because we live and move in this sea of energy we are sending and receiving qualities of vibration all the time. For example, if you walk into a crowd of strangers you sense the warmth radiated to you from across the room when someone sends you a heartfelt smile. You likewise sense the vibratory quality and impact when someone shoots you a look that could kill.

By understanding the energy that predominates in our makeup and the energy makeup of people around us we can learn how to balance and blend the energies within ourselves and interpersonally in a very practical way.

Our specific interest and focus here is in the tremendous insight we may gain by learning to recognize, balance and blend the energies between ourselves and our mates.

One formalized system for understanding energy is the energy of The Seven Rays, as introduced by Dr. Michael D. Robbins.[17] Even though I now do seminars on understanding energy, which includes the energy of the Seven Rays, I had not studied this particular system on the way to finding my Soulmate. Formal study came some time after I met my Soulmate.

Will it be helpful for you to formally study more about energy? I think the answer is both yes and no. No, in the sense that foremost, I re-emphasize, that your most powerful tool is the use of your own inner wisdom and intuitive sight to guide you on the way to finding your Soulmate. These w ill enable you to recognize and to know who is right for you. Again, revelations about your Soulmate will come after deep Soul searching, incessant prayer, meditation and time spent in deep contemplation on your own qualities of energy and on the qualities of energy you want in a mate.

However, Yes, in the sense that formal study of an energy system may assist you in attuning to the qualities of energy you are attracted to and compatible with long before you meet your Soulmate. This kind of attention to energy will aid you in recognizing your Soulmate when he or she appears. As well, increased understanding of the different qualities of energy aids you in appreciating all types, which is beneficial to any relationship.

When we have found our Soulmate we are with someone who we are connected with on a Soul-to-Soul level. Understanding energy is understanding the Soul note that is sounded when we came into incarnation. Finding our Soulmate is finding someone with the same or complementary energy.

Energy springs from the *One eternal source* and differentiates into subsidiary streams of energy which have their influence on all life and give quality to that life in its varied expressions. Different groups of people throughout the ages call these qualities of energy by different names. For example, it may be called deities, Gods, Orishas, Rays, Principles, Virtues and Vices, Powers, Traits, Psychological Types, and so on.

This energy is cloaked by different groups in different garments of beliefs or thoughts which enables them to see this energy embodied and animated. A whole system of stories, practices, prayer, rituals, etc., are employed to recognize, profile, classify, invoke, and to give reverence to these energies. These energies characterize us, giving certain qualities to you and me. Certain of these energies dominate your makeup while others are less demonstrated in your makeup. As such, those energies that dominate your energy makeup become part of your line of least resistance, meaning you express these energies with ease.

The energy of the Seven Rays describes seven discrete streams of energy that qualify life in its myriad forms. Within each stream there are qualities of energy. These qualities of energy may be expressed at a higher turn of the spiral or used positively, at its most optimal and divine level of expression. We would experience a human's (or other entity's such as a couple, a group, nation, planet, etc.) strengths when energy is being used in this way. These qualities of energy may also be expressed at a lower turn of the spiral or used negatively, thus demonstrating the weaknesses of a human (or other entity).

For example, Ray 1 is <u>Power and Will</u>. Some of the qualities of strength in expressing this energy at the higher turn of the spiral are courage, strong sense of purpose, the power to lead, direct and govern. This energy moves in a one pointed, straight line direction with force, power, and purpose.

On a lower turn of the spiral this same energy becomes aggression, domination, control, and cruelty. So we can see that when this energy is expressed positively or spiraled up it may be the energy of a dynamic, principled, and courageous leader. This same energy spiraled downward and used negatively becomes the energy of an unprincipled and egotistical bully. Again, one may express Ray 1 energy as part of their energy or Ray makeup. While others who do not readily express this energy may invoke it or call forth its expression by taking assertiveness training, for example.

Another example is Ray 2, <u>Love and Wisdom</u>. Some of the strengths of this Ray are loving wisdom, exquisite sensitivity and inclusiveness. This is the Ray of the teacher. At a higher turn of the spiral or used positively, someone expressing this energy would be able to show great empathy, warmth and sensitivity toward another. They would be able to stand in the other's shoes and assess the other's need. Understanding the needs, he or she is able to teach.

However, at a lower turn of the spiral, sensitivity can become oversensitivity, vulnerability, and fear of impact from the world around. These individuals have a need to withdraw and retreat to self protect. Someone who feels so keenly sensitive may feel keenly vulnerable to being wounded. This is someone who may have trouble saying no, and becomes a doormat for others. Instead of sharing their wisdom, they may withdraw into aloofness with their many books and display coldness. To call in this ray, one may take sensitivity training for example.

In turn, each ray may be understood in terms of its strengths and weaknesses. You can begin to see how you would get a different picture of someone depending on how and what qualities are being expressed.

It is also important to understand the human constitution which briefly includes the following vehicles or bodies and their function:

Physical/etheric body
the energy of the
physical form, vitality

We have differing levels of flexibility, strength, stamina and grace. We know we do not all have the same physical makeup and vitality for example. Some people require eight hours of sleep and are likely to feel sluggish if they do not get their usual amount of rest (Ray 7). Others are able to go and go without much sleep and without particularly paying much attention to any set rituals of going to sleep or getting up (Ray 3).

Emotional body
the energy of
feelings and desires

According to their ray energy some people may be emotionally reactive (Ray 6), while others can be more serene and calm (Ray 2). Still others may be volcanic in their emotional expression (Ray 1), holding things in for a time, then erupting and letting things out.

Mental body
the energy of mind,
how we think, reason, plan

We know that there are differences in how people think. For example, some think in terms of logic and concepts and in a linear manner (Ray 5), while others are imaginative and think more in terms of metaphor and analogy (Ray 4).

Personality
how we get our act together
and keep it together

This is the energy that coordinates the physical, emotional, and mental bodies so that these work in a purposeful way. You may awake in the morning to find that your mind is going in one direction, your emotions in another, and your body frankly does not feel like going at all. It is the energy of the personality that actually qualifies how you get your act together and get out of the door to do something meaningful in the world or to at least attempt to take care of your personal sphere of existence and its attendant needs. So if you have a 6th ray personality, for example, the energy of great vision, inspiration, devotion, and commitment to ideals (such as the work ethic) will all influence how you move. The personality is the instrument which the Soul works through.

Soul
the Light within

The ray energy of your Soul indicates your Higher purpose, meaning, and reason for being. Some people incarnate with the express purpose of being leaders (ray 1), teachers (ray 2), artists (ray 4), or scientists (ray 5) for example. It is in knowing the ray energy of your soul that you are able to understand more clearly the work that you have come into the world to do.

Again, the Soul is the Higher Self which seeks more and more to imbue our daily life with wisdom, intelligent living, and selfless love. It guides you to perform a service in the world that is larger than your limited personal sphere of existence and is in accord with the Divine Will and Purpose for your life.

Briefly stated, it is important to understand that there are Seven Rays and Five Vehicles, or bodies, through which these energies may be expressed. Each vehicle is qualified by a Ray.

THE SEVEN RAYS

Ray 1   Power & Will

Ray 2   Love & Wisdom

Ray 3   Active Intelligence

Ray 4   Harmony Through Conflict

Ray 5   Concrete Knowledge & Science

Ray 6   Devotion & Abstract Idealism

Ray 7   Order & Ceremonial Magic

THE FIVE VEHICLES

Soul

Personality

Mental

Emotional/Astral

Physical/Etheric

1.   These five vehicles or bodies are each qualified by a particular Ray energy. These bodies or vehicles which make up the human constitution and the ray energy that qualifies them become points of contact between you and your mate. An example of an energy formula follows:

◆   **Ray 2 Soul**

■   *Ray 6 Personality*

☐   Ray 4 Mental

☐   Ray 2 Emotional/Astral

☐   Ray 7 Physical/Etheric vehicle

As these points are active and alive within you, you will want to make these points of connection with your mate. You will also want to gain clarity on why you are not connecting.

2.   The energy formula of your mate may be very similar or very different from your own. These similarities or differences will effect how you interact together. For example, I often observe in doing couples therapy that couples get into a blame game over the qualities of energy each partner expresses. For example, he says, "I wish she would be more interested in the details of our finances." She says, "He does not know how to loosen up, have fun and be more spontaneous." In this instance, he is wishing his mate would express more 3rd and 5th ray energy like himself, while she wishes he would be more like her and express more 4th and 2nd ray energy.

Each partner can teach the other what comes naturally and easily for him or her, rather than blame one another for those qualities that are not easily expressed. Couples can compliment the energy makeup of each other while learning to invoke more of the qualities of energies that each needs in order to live more fully.

Your mate can role model those energies you most need to cultivate in your own makeup. *That your mate expresses particular energies has contributed to your attraction to him or her in the first instance.* Instead of coming to blame our mates for the very qualities that attracted us to them we can praise and appreciate the qualities they possess. Allow your mate to teach you and allow yourself to teach your mate. You can learn from the valuable role modeling your mate does of particular qualities of energy. This will aid you to incorporate these qualities more into your makeup.

One partner may get locked into being the one to express particular qualities of energy, like assertiveness (ray 1), patience (ray 2), orderliness (ray 7), or vision for the future (ray 6). These may not come easily for the other partner, who may make no effort to cultivate these qualities. At the same time, by always taking the lead, the partner with these qualities may inhibit the cultivation of these qualities in his or her mate.

Likewise you may also feel locked into a particular pattern of energy expression that is hindering expressing of your full energy potential. This is true particularly if your mate (and others) is depending on you to continue to express yourself in a certain way. Problems arise when couples come to feel they are no longer balancing, blending, complimenting, and learning from each others energy formulas.

3.   No matter what your Ray energy makeup is, or your mate's, you can both work more consciously together to spiral up and express your qualities of energy positively instead of negatively. In this way you are working to express qualities of energy at their most optimal or divine level.

4.   One can focus their awareness in one vehicle more than the others. For example, one may be more focused in the physical or emotional vehicles and less in the mental, personality or Soul vehicle. You can see how the quality of life expressed would differ depending upon how expanded or limited is one's focus of awareness.

Some relationships for example involve the contact of two people below the diaphragm. This means that their connection is mostly concerned with sharing the creature comforts of food, shelter, sexual pleasure and meeting desires. These are relationships of survival with little focus on the higher plan and purpose for the lives of the couple.

As we attune to and coordinate the energy of our own instrument, we are guided more by the energy of our Soul. Our consciousness is more expanded and we can relate to another in a more expanded way. In return, we want to be related to in a more expanded way also. To be in a relationship which fails to recognize all of who we are causes us a sense of pain and truncation. As we journey along our path, our personality vehicle or instrument becomes more integrated and attuned to the Light of the Soul.

Through a process of soul infusion we truly become souls that have a personality instrument through which divine purpose may be expressed on earth, and not just personalities who may make an occasional reference to having a soul. This can happen at varying rates as each partner unfolds at their own pace into greater Self awareness. Partners can consciously aid one another in this process.

EXERCISE

Understanding Your Own
And A Potential Mate's Energy

See Appendix 1 for a listing of
qualities of the Seven Ray energies.

Write down the qualities you express.

Meditate upon these qualities
so that you may become more
attuned to them and to discover
how you may spiral them upward
so that these energies are
expressed positively.

Next, write down and meditate
upon the qualities of energy
you seek in a mate.

Imagine both of your energies
balancing and blending
together harmoniously.

You must steep yourself in these energies through your meditation, prayer, and affirmation. Create that Sacred space within, clear the blockages through releasing and forgiving, and do the hard work needed to enhance your self esteem and to heal. Through these efforts, you will be well on the way to a deep Universal attunement that will put you on line with your own Soul contact and that of your Soulmate.

The attunement with your own Soul will open you to the abundance and prosperity that the Universe has in store for you. *Just one of the many blessings of this attunement will be the increased awareness and connection with the Soul of the mate who is divinely and perfectly suited for you spiritually, mentally, emotionally, and physically.*

NOTES

Chapter Nine

How To Recognize
Who Is A Soulmate

August 29, 1985

Dear God,
   I have loved you from the cradle, I will
love you to the grave. I will love you for all
eternity.

AFFIRMATION

Expressing Appreciation

I give thanks for Divine guidance.
I give praise to the All In All,
the One, that I may be of service.
I am appreciating life and all of its Divine
blessings. There is a continual
prayer of thanksgiving on my lips.

August 30, 1985

Dear God, Father of My Soul,
   I remember what my spiritual friend
(Donald) said about my search for my
Soulmate. He said, "Just go along, doing
your work in the world and when you
least expect it you will look up and there
he will be."

I held onto his words sensing how true they would become one day.

STEP 43

Recognizing Who Is Your Soulmate

Donald is a very dear spiritual friend. He and I have a very strong spiritual connection. Our relationship is non-romantic and non-sexual. I met Donald while still in my first marriage, and he filled some of the void I felt. He mirrored those spiritual and mental parts of me that had been unmirrored for years in my first marriage. Donald and I have a spiritual intimacy that many would not understand. He has touched me so deeply here. He once gave me a book to read. When I opened it and began reading its pages the tears began to stream down my face. The book spoke so deeply to my Soul. How did he know to give me this book? At the time, no one on earth, not even my own mother would have known to give me this book, nor how deeply it would touch me.

Through our communion, we look deeply into our reason and meaning for being. We try to find answers to life's mysteries and to understand the parts we are to play in this life drama. Often we are able to communicate without words and we need only to send out the thought and heartfelt impulse to one another for each to respond by calling the other on the telephone.

Donald and I both have a second Ray Soul, that of teacher and healer. One may say that Donald is a Soulmate. In many ways he is because of our Soul-to-Soul connection. We share a strong spiritual bond, but we are not what I consider *True Soulmates.* Donald and I share in our life purposes by supporting one another in our service on the planet. He enhances my life purpose and I enhance his. As a spiritual friend he has been *a mate to my Soul.*

If we are fortunate we will meet many mates to our Soul in our lifetime. Many are experiencing these special kinds of Soul connections with a friend, a grandmother, a teacher, and so on. Some may feel a Soulmate union exists between those who share a common purpose. I feel this is true. However when I use the term Soulmate, or true Soulmate, I am referring to a union that is consummated spiritually and sexually.

I opened to noticing within myself (even though this was not an option) that I have not wanted to share a physical plane connection with Donald. I have not felt a physical or sexual attraction to Donald, nor the kind of emotional connection I need in a mate. I am very fulfilled with our relationship as it is without any wish to explore these dimensions. I even feel that sharing a physical/ sexual dimension would have detracted rather than enhanced what we have together as spiritual friends. I love him dearly, but it is not a romantic love.

Finding a spiritual friend who vibrated on the same soul ray as I did, did not fill the void or take away my longing for my Soulmate, rather, it intensified it. All relationships teach us something about ourselves and bring us information about the approach of our Soulmate. We can spot the approach of our Soulmate as parts of ourselves are awakened and reflected in our relationship with others.

My spiritual relationship with my friend moved me to both ask the question and to affirm 'yes' within myself—wouldn't it be wonderful to share this type of depth of connection with a mate in marriage? I wanted more and more to share these aspects of myself with a mate I could commit to spending my life with. Again, for me a Soulmate is that one with whom I can share every aspect of who I am. In choosing a mate, it is just as important to find someone you feel a physical and emotional connection with as it is a mental and spiritual one. Donald and I have known each other in other lifetimes. I feel in the lifetimes we have shared we have always walked the courtyard together in deep communion and discussion about the ageless wisdom—the ancient mysteries.

STEP 44

Recording Your Dreams

September 15, 1985

Dear God,
In a dream last night I saw myself in union with the energy of my Soulmate. It was a beautiful union. I know this dream means that I will experience physical union with my Soulmate soon.

Dreams are portals to connect on the Soul level. Do you keep a journal? Do you record your dreams? Dreams bring important messages about the approach of your Soulmate. They bring awareness of your readiness to unite with your Soulmate.

STEP 45

Analyzing What Other Encounters Are Revealing To You About The Approach Of Your Soulmate

Four other men who came into my life on my way to finding my Soulmate are in need of mention. Each time I agonized, is this him? Each was a brief encounter. The first was a man I met in 1969, shortly after meeting Jay. His name was Bill. We made a very strong and intense spiritual connection and this felt like a Soulmate connection. He lived in another state and his time in the state in which I resided was brief. After just one week of knowing one another he asked me to go with him when he returned to his hometown. I felt torn. My family was in the same state in which I lived. I was in school and had a strong aspiration to pursue my education and, even though Jay and I were in the early beginning stages of our relationship, I knew Jay cared deeply about me and I needed the emotional and physical security of that relationship. I told Bill no. I chose to remain where I was.

For years afterwards I thought about him. Lingering in those years that followed was that *special feeling* I felt when I had been with Bill last. Over the years, my imaginings of my Soulmate often assumed the face of this man. After my separation from Jay, I invoked the powers of the Universe to see Bill again. I needed to get clarity and closure on this relationship. Although brief, this was an encounter that had a major impact and profound effect upon me.

Perhaps there is someone that you too have had a brief encounter with yet felt a powerful attraction and strong connection between you. Then, this person moved out of your life space. Perhaps this is a high school sweetheart or someone you chatted with while in a supermarket or waiting for the bus. Perhaps this is a true Soulmate connection. Perhaps not.

A lot of fantasy may be built around a brief connection with another man or woman that has not yet been tested by the daily challenges involved in relationship building on the physical, emotional, mental, personality and spiritual levels.

Because energy follows thought, each time you think of this person you are energizing huge thoughtforms about him or her that hover around you. Your energy becomes bounded in these thoughtforms. For this reason as well as others, it is important to get more information and closure on these relationships, if possible.

EXERCISE

Getting Closure On Past
(Other) Relationships If Possible

Determine if this relationship can be
prospered and moved forward, deepening
a romantic connection and commitment
in the world of reality, rather than just in
your mind in the realm of imaginings.

You may invoke the Universe for a meeting
that brings the two of you across the gulf
of time and space. Perhaps you can write a
letter or even call, if this would not
create too much disturbance in your lives.

If you determine that there is *no* possibility of fur-
thering a real earthly plane union then you may consider the option to release and to let go of this connection so that your energy may be freed to seek a union
that is attainable. Always allow Spirit to guide you in the
process of knowing when to hold on or when to release
and let go in relationships.

EXERCISE

**Exploring The Connections
With The One In Your Midst**

Ask yourself the following three questions:

First, Is there someone else in my life space
that I could be sharing my life with?

Second, Does my focus on the one who is
absent, or who has not as yet appeared in my
life, keep me from recognizing this person?

Third, Am I missing an opportunity to
cultivate a Soul to Soul relationship with
this other being who is right in my midst?

Remember everything has the potential for Soul's
growth. Lastly, there may be deeper spiritual meaning
hidden in the song title that says, "If You Can't Be With
The One You Love, Love The One You Are With." Remember nothing is ever wasted. By loving someone who does
not exactly love you in the way you need to be loved you
may still be:

1.   Fulfilling your spiritual need to love another and fulfilling the spiritual need of the other to be loved.

2.   Learning valuable lessons in compassion and understanding.

3.   Moving closer to that one who you will love and who will love you in a God-like way.

Each relationship is an opportunity to experience a greater expanse in loving and in being loved by another. Each relationship is but a rehearsal in learning to love unconditionally and universally.

How do I understand the event of meeting Bill on my path? I understand this event in two ways. Either Bill was a Soulmate and I have had the good fortune to encounter more than one Soulmate in this lifetime, even though I had been unwilling to seize the opportunity at the time. Or, he was a man on my path, like my friend Donald, who blessed me by strumming some ancient chords within me, allowing me to remember the vibration of what Divine Soulmate unions feel like. *As a messenger of love, he enhanced my journey by heralding and awakening my consciousness to the potential for deep spiritual unions in mates on earth.* If he were not the *object* then he reminded me of my *Ideal.* He unveiled the archetype. With my memory awakened he increased my longing and pointed the way—On My Way To Finding My Soulmate.

Dear God,
    For this I give thanks to Bill.

I invoked the Universe to bring Bill and me together so that closure could be made. I needed to determine whether the relationship could be moved forward, or if I needed to reclaim the energy that had vitalized the thought forms of this man off and on for over seventeen years.

Just prior to meeting my true Soulmate, the Universe responded and brought Bill and me together for a chance meeting. Our moments together were absolutely wonderful! But we both realized that our lives had taken us in different directions. I knew when we parted that I was not likely to see him again in this lifetime. The last words I spoke to him were, "I will look for you in the next lifetime." I knew that I would want to encounter this energy again in another life, even if we were just friends or co-workers. His vibration, his energy, just having known him has had a very positive effect on my life.

Dear God,

Today I am really saying good-bye to you Bill. Our paths crossed briefly many years ago. In an instant the feelings were strong, the attraction was intense. Then you were gone from my path, taken miles away in a different direction.

You have been a flower on my path. A wonderful, beautiful blossom that stirred my Soul at first glance. I have returned to your memory often.

I now release you Bill, I let you go, you are free. I release you to your highest and greatest good, may you go in peace. You release me to my highest and greatest good. May I go in peace.

I give thanks to the Creator for the lessons learned and the wonderful time we spent together in this sacred encounter.

Letting Bill go after all those years freed up an abundance of energy. This energy cleared away blockages or drags in my energy field and hastened the precipitation of my actual meeting of my Soulmate on the earthly plane.

Spirit informed me that this full release was absolutely necessary for my happiness! I could not continue to visualize and vitalize a memory, and at the same time visualize and vitalize union with my Soulmate. *Allow Spirit to inform you of the good and perfect thing to do in each instance as you make your way to finding your Soulmate.*

The other three men who came into my life space also taught me something about the process of finding my Soulmate and actually hastened the process for me. I realized these men had physically reminded me of Bill, and that I had been attracted to men who had certain physical features. For example, I like tall men. I am 5' 8"; my first husband was 6' 3". When I met my Soulmate Lester, I discovered that he was 5' 10". I am also physically attracted to men with a certain shape of eyes. These physical attractions sound so shallow as I write about them now, yet this physical composite had a strong pull on me.

Each of these men taught me I had to let go of this rigid and exacting composite of external appearance because it was getting in the way of meeting my Soulmate. This composite formed a haze over my ability to see clearly and needed to be dissipated. Furthermore, if there was nothing behind this image, or if the man who donned such a physical garment and I could make no other connection, then what did this really matter?

Russ Michaels says on this subject that, "the face that our personality wears in the world is far different than the beautiful countenance of the Soul."[18] Remember, the personality consists of the physical, emotional and mental bodies, or how we appear, feel, and think. The energy of the Soul is what draws us beyond the form aspect to a deeper level of recognition and connection.

STEP 46

Letting Go Of Fitting Your
Soulmate Into A Rigid Image

Dear God,
But now I must give up this image. It is
substance that I seek. It is an enlightened
spiritual man that I seek union with. I am
on the right track, closing in!

I felt these experiences were really guiding me and
providing me with needed clarity in recognizing my
Soulmate when the time came for us to unite in a real
earthly plane encounter. I sensed that time and space
were narrowing, drawing us closer to the place of actually meeting face to face. Although I had to deal with the
fallen hope and disappointment of these other encounters along the way, I felt a tremendous joyfulness about
what Spirit was revealing to me.

After sorting these experiences through I had the distinct sense of being put back on track and nearing the
goal. It is through these experiences that we are able to
sort out that which has been our *programming* about
what a mate should look like on the outside. Once you
do this you can focus more clearly on the essence or the
essential qualities you seek to find on the inside of your
mate.

EXERCISE

Examining How You Have Been
Programmed In Selecting A Mate

Please ponder upon the following question:

What has been your programming
culturally, socially or otherwise,
that has conditioned your attraction
to a potential mate?

Make a list of the rigid images you hold.

If you feel these are getting in the way
of recognizing your Soulmate
then say the following, as I did,
to release yourself of these images:

Dear God,
I release these images, I let them go.
I release you, images, I let you go.
I release you, false images and
false objects, I let you go!

Journal Continued ...
   I had no one to blame but me on Fri-
day—sitting there like a bump on a log on
a date with Sam. I was letting myself be
attracted to his image instead of keeping
my search from the inside outward.

As you attune more to the qualities of energy you would like in a mate you will move from a superficial level of attraction to one that touches the very essence of him or her.

NOTES

NOTES

Chapter Ten

A Soulmate Meditation: Visualization, Prayer, And Invoking Him Or Her

September 21, 1985

Dear God,
    Again I call out deep within my Soul to my Soulmate. It is curious that just the thought of him being near brings me such peace, such joy. This morning I lay in bed feeling very still and serene in my thoughts of my Soulmate.

Doing meditation and visualization steeps you in the vibration and remembrance of your Soulmate's energy, so that recognition is possible when you meet on the physical plane. It is so joyful to sit within these gentle, soothing, and life promoting vibrations.

STEP 47

**Clarifying What You
Want In A Soulmate**

Dear God,
*   The man I seek union with is warm,*
loving and caring. He is someone who
looks deeply within himself and questions
himself on how to do his best and live life
to the fullest. He is someone who has a
deep connection with God, and like myself,
recognizes himself to be a Co-worker and
Co-creator in the Great Divine Plan to
bring heaven to earth.
*   He is someone in his 40's, someone who*
has been married and divorced, has ado-
lescent or adult children and an estab-
lished career. He possesses mental clarity
and keen intelligence. He is able to pro-
cess the Universe with me.
*   We are both seekers of truth and we use*
our spiritual and mental ability to discern
the highest and greatest good.

Little did I know then when I imagined what my
Soulmate would be like how close I was in my vision of
him. It is important to see or visualize what you want in
hastening your union with your Soulmate.

EXERCISE

**Asking For What You
Want In A Soulmate**

Invoke the Universe for
what you want in a mate.

Speak to each level in terms of what you
desire in a Soulmate spiritually, mentally,
emotionally, and physically.

Be clear on what you ask the Universe for.
Write in your journal the physical,
emotional, mental and spiritual
qualities you desire in a mate.

Meditate on these qualities and
experience these energies as very
enlivened in your meditation.

After deciding what you want in a Soulmate, it is important to say, "Thy Will Be Done." Then Let Go and Let God. Again, It is important not to focus too rigidly on some feature you would like in a Soulmate, particularly physical features, which are generally the most pronounced or underpronounced upon first meeting a mate. This can interfere with your recognition of your true

Soulmate. Your Soulmate may be under your nose, right there in your midst. Yet you may fail to recognize him or her because you are set on union with someone, for example, who has a certain type of hair, body build, education, fellowship with a particular group, standing in the community and so on.

I knew that I visualized a man with an African-American body, and who would possess a consciousness of the African experience, but I also knew I must remain open to the Divine outworking of the Universe. I would learn later from my Soulmate, who is African American, that he was leery of light complexion Black women like myself, and had specifically avoided dating them. He felt relationships with them would be more problematic than relationships with darker complexion Black women, for a whole host of reasons. He was reflecting some of the racial history that is a legacy from slavery and we had to work this through. This is another example of how rigid images may be held and need to be released on both sides.

STEP 48

Meditating, Visualizing, Praying And Invoking

There is a beautiful tree-lined pond that I would go to in the process of invoking the Universe for this sacred union. I would sit on a rock by the water's edge meditating and praying my earnest prayers. I would talk to my Soulmate letting him know that I was waiting for him. I would see us together in a blissful union of activity. I knew that of all the men in the Universe he was the one for me.

Through your meditation on your Soulmate you become deeply steeped in the feel and qualities of both of your energies together. By meditating on your Soulmate you may experience the marvelous intermingling of the qualities of energy you both radiate in a wonderful, magical and harmonious blend.

SOULMATE MEDITATION

Connecting With Your Soulmate
Before You Meet

Sit with your eyes closed
and take some deep breaths,
cleansing within and clearing
the space around you.

Breath in a sense of peace and ease.
Breath out any sense of lack or limitation.
Feel your physical body relax.

Experience a stillness and calmness
of your emotional body.
Imagine the emotions like a still, clear pond.

Allow yourself to experience clarity
in your mind or mental body.

Ask yourself, How do I love, and
how do I desire to be loved in return?

Ponder this question for a few moments.

Now imagine a brilliant light above your head.
This is the light of the Soul.
From your head to your toes, experience your
whole being infused with this brilliant light.

Feel a sense of boundlessness and bliss
as you fully enter into Soul consciousness.
Step into this Light and
stand fully in the Spiritual realm.

Now imagine you are walking through a misty
garden. Even through the mist you can
see this garden to be exquisitely beautiful,
lush, and sweet smelling.

As you continue to walk you begin
to feel a familiar presence in your midst.

You now become aware of a brilliant light
which is the Soul light of your Soulmate.
See the light of this Soul approaching the
light of your Soul and feel the growing
warmth and intensity in this approach.

Experience the bliss of this
Soul-to-Soul union with your Soulmate.
Feel your hearts well with the joy you both
feel at this divine, sacred, encounter.

Feel the electricity that flows between you,
setting aglow every fiber of your being and feel
the pull of the magnetism that now draws you
both ever together, as it has across other
lifetimes, through eternity.

See yourselves move in a joyous cosmic
dance. As you look deeply into one another,
communicate the fullness of your hearts.

Tell your Soulmate that you are so grateful for
this union on the Soul level, and that you
await the time when you may experience this
union precipitated on the physical plane.

Spend time with your Soulmate.
Your beloved.
That one you love and who loves you
completely, physically, emotionally,
mentally, and spiritually.
The one you perfectly reflect and contain,
and in whom you are
perfectly reflected and contained.

Steep in the energies of your Soulmate union.

Say to him or her,
My Dear Soulmate,
it is through your tender recognition and
reflection of my being and divine qualities
that you strum my remembrance of
my reason, meaning, and purpose in being.

By reflecting my Divine qualities,
you strum my remembrance of
my image and likeness of God.

I look within you and behold
my own Divinity and yours.

You aid and strengthen my
sense of life purpose.

Together we are help mates
who aid each other to play our part
with aspiration and firm commitment in the
Great Divine plan to bring heaven to earth.

My Dear Soulmate,
I return now to the outer realm
with the sweetness of our time spent
in deep communion together
now pervading my every thought.

Joy is overflowing in my heart.
I give thanks to the Creator
for this experience.

Our Souls are intertwined whether or not
we are currently sharing earth life together.
We always have access to one another
through the portal of our Soul contact.

May Spirit move to precipitate us both
in time and space and in union on the earthly
plane so that what is felt invisibly may be
seen, touched, and grasped on earth.

Feel the joy in your heart
as you expand how you love.
Feel the excitement in every
fiber of your being now aglow
with a zest for life and living!

NOTES

NOTES

Chapter Eleven

Completing All The Steps
In Manifesting This Event

September 24, 1985

Dear God, Father, Mother of My Soul,
I will soon be with my Soulmate. We
will soon be united. I yearn for him and I
know he yearns for me. I merely need to
continue with the work I have already
begun and our paths will naturally be led
to one another. I will soon be with my
Soulmate. He is inwardly searching for me
and I for him.
I know not what he looks like but I will
recognize him by looking deeply into his
eyes and seeing myself there within. Our
Souls will connect.

On a deep level I knew the time was drawing near for
my Soulmate and me to unite. I felt I knew him intimately on the spiritual plane and I merely needed to wait
for the unseen to manifest on the physical plane. I knew
this event would precipitate soon, just as rain is precipitated from the fullness of the clouds above, when they
achieve a certain ripeness.

September 25, 1985

Dear God,
    I have asked you what the formula is. I am not able to give up the desire. So far I am not able to satisfy it. I have tried deeply to figure out the way. I am feeling I have exhausted my resources. ...

In my deepest communion with God I asked, "Reveal to me what else needs to be done? What remains undone to hasten my union?" I was feeling impatient. At this point I felt that I had done all I knew to do. I had responded to all that was revealed for me to do by Spirit.

    Journal continued ...
    I will sit at the temple and wait for my beloved, my Soulmate. I seek to connect with the most highly evolved place in him. Therefore, I await at the place I know to be the most highly evolved [place in me] that our Souls may attract.

    According to Michaels, "Soul attraction occurs only at Soul levels. The Soul never descends below the levels of abstract mind. Only the highest thoughts, feelings, or personal vibrations can touch and move the Soul of another into reciprocal response."[19]

Journal continued ...
    In the meantime I affirm: I am absolute
faith in God. I am infinite love for my
fellow man and woman, for all beings. I
am selflessness, helping others to reach
their goal.

I realized that I had to get the thought of finding my Soulmate off of my mind. It was continually on my mind and I realized at that point that it was interfering with my being fully present in my work. Besides, it was uncomfortable to keep thinking over and over about an event, particularly since I felt I had done and was doing all I knew to do to hasten that event.

STEP 49

Letting Go
And Letting God

There came a point when I felt the process was nearly complete. A time when I knew I had done the *inner work* of manifesting this event. Yet as much as I thought I had done all I knew to do—on my way to finding my Soulmate —Spirit revealed to me that which remained undone. That was the step of completely letting go and letting God. As much as I thought I had, I had not *completely let go!*

A poem that I came across in my journey captures this moment:

Let Go & Let God

As children bring their broken toys with tears for us to mend, I brought my broken dreams to God, because he was my friend.

But then instead of leaving Him in peace to work alone, I hung around and tried to help with ways that were my own.

At last I snatched them back and cried, "How can you be so slow?" "My child," He said, "What could I do?' You never did let go."

When Spirit spoke to me at this point I immediately went to a cabinet in my kitchen. I took out a small basket that had a lid on top that I had been using as a sewing basket. I quickly emptied out its contents and entered into my sacred space in my home and again went into deep communion with God. I lit a candle and an incense and on a three by five index card I wrote the following:

October 2, 1985

Dear God,
    I place this basket on the altar. Therein
this basket I place all my desires for
spiritual, mental, emotional, and physical
union with my Soulmate, my beloved.
    I let go of this basket into your hands
Dear God, Father of My Soul, for safe
keeping and in faith, Father, that you will
work the miracle that I cannot. In faith
that you will unite me and my Soulmate in
our deepest love for one another, forever
after.
    In the meantime, I continue with my
work in the world in peace, unperturbed,
and without distraction.

                              Love,
                              Terri

I gently and lovingly folded this card up and placed it in the basket. I put the lid on top then placed the basket on the windowsill in my bedroom. *At this point I turned everything completely over to God and fully put all thoughts out of my mind.*

I felt a tremendous relief! I felt the process was complete and that I had done the work and all I needed to do now was to just continue in my daily service as I had tried to do all along the way. I had done and was continuing to do the work of preparing myself to meet my Soulmate.

STEP 50

The Invisible Becomes Visible— We Meet At Last

Michael Ross says that, "You will meet your Soulmate doing the most mundane of tasks." [20]

On Christmas eve, December 24, 1985, I was in the Laundromat doing my laundry. It has been a practice of mine to always carry something to read and generally this is something of a spiritual or inspirational nature. On the cover of the book that I was reading at that time was a rather chubby yogi master sitting in lotus position and clad in just a loin cloth.

I did not see *him* first. He saw me. He was caught by the cover of the book I was reading. (Later, I would learn that from the angle he was looking at the book cover he was thinking, "That looks like a porno book she is reading." He was asking himself, "Why is this attractive woman reading this book in public. I have got to say something to her.") "Excuse me," he said, "What are you doing reading a book like that?"

"What do you mean?" I asked. I held the book out so that he could see it more closely. When he saw the cover he seemed embarrassed but quickly recovered. He told me what he had been thinking. We both began to laugh. He told me his name was Lester, and asked my name.

Given the subject of the book, we began a conversation about things of a spiritual nature. After talking very passionately about this subject for quite a while, we paused and looked deeply at one another. In that moment we both realized that neither of us could have had that sort of conversation everyday and certainly not with just anyone. We connected on the spiritual plane.

Having only one small bag, Lester finished his laundry sooner than I did. I seemingly had tons of it. As he surveyed my laundry he quietly wondered how many children I had.

He asked me for my telephone number, and he gave me his. He began calling me frequently and we talked for hours and hours on the telephone. A strong connection began to develop between us spiritually, mentally, and emotionally. He was very warm and sensitive and he loved to talk and share his ideas about life. He was profoundly affected by human events and had tremendous compassion for all beings. He also had a wonderful sense of humor, as I quickly discovered from our initial encounter! I loved the way he thought, probed and reflected deeply upon life and sought to understand the inner and outer workings of the world around him, as I did.

Lester asked me repeatedly when we would see each other again. I kept putting him off. Even when he came into my life space I did not accept this event right away. I even rejected it. I told him of my recent separation and that I was not sure if I was ready for a new relationship.

I could not believe myself as I uttered these words through the telephone! Yet some fears around involvement had cropped up that I had not quite anticipated. I was struggling with being a single parent and working full time in my profession. Questions arose for me like where was I going to find the time to cultivate this relationship? I said to him, "We are enjoying talking on the telephone, we are developing a wonderful friendship and why didn't we just leave it at that."

He told me, "I am deeply interested in you and feel a strong inner connection with you and besides, you're attractive." He let me know we could not possibly remain just "telephone" friends. He continued by saying, "I have known some progressive, highly functioning people in my life, but then something happens to them and they never recover and they even begin to lose ground. I hear you have had a separation, but you must move on."

STEP 51

Recognizing Your Soulmate
When You Meet

He really got my attention with these words. Who was this man anyway! He was not a psychotherapist, I was. Yet he always spoke with such wisdom. There was a further stirring deep within me. I decided to go out with him and so we planned our first date. We were to meet in a Friendly's restaurant for his birthday.

When I walked in he was already seated. As we sat together drinking coffee I noted how interested I was in him. I felt excited in his presence, not ecstatic, but excited.

As we sat across from each other talking and looking into one another's eyes, we both had our hands on the table. Suddenly we began to play with each other's fingers. *In that very instant of touching his hands and feeling him touching mine I felt this incredible surge of energy throughout my entire body!* I remembered this as the energy in all my dreams, visions and imaginings. It was the energy from the misty past. It was the energy of my Soulmate, a vibration I knew well.

His energy was electric in that it touched every fiber of my being. It was magnetic in that it instantaneously drew me closer to him. My heart began to open to him. My consciousness was suddenly flooded with the memories of all the times I had spent with this same energy.

In those moments that energy had given me a sense of peace, comfort, and ease as it did now in this moment. But now this energy was embodied and had taken real form, and HE was now sitting across from me! I now felt ECSTATIC. I was filled with a sense of joy that I could now locate him in time and space, that *I could REACH OUT AND TOUCH HIM.*

Later in our relationship there would be many times when I would take my index finger, reach out and touch Lester playfully. Each time I would do this I was reminded of all the times before we met when I could not touch him nor locate him physically in time and space. I would be filled with the wonder and awe of now being able to do so. I would engage often in this joyful play with that *mysterious boundary between the visible and the invisible.*

I gave him a copy of, <u>As A Man Thinketh</u>, as a birthday present. I noticed he had the most sensitive eyes. "How tall are you?" I asked. He leaned forward and said confidently, "Don't worry we fit." I knew he meant fit on all levels, physically, mentally, emotionally and spiritually. To this day we spend a lot of time looking deeply into each other's eyes. We touch noses together and just stay there looking into one another's Souls.

I had car trouble that night so Lester offered to follow my car to make sure I got home safely. Two blocks away from my house I pulled over. Seeing me stop, he pulled over also. I was a cautious woman and even though he had asked, he still did not know my address. He got out of his car and walked over to mine. After standing outside surveying my car for a moment he assured me that I would make it the rest of the way home.

It was winter time and he looked cold standing out there so I opened the door and he got into my car where we sat talking for a while longer. He asked, "Can I sit nearer to you?" as he slid over in the seat before I could answer. Then in a very sincere voice, one that I felt certain I had heard before from the misty past, he said, "I want to make you happy. Will you let me make you happy?"

With these words I felt a tremendous sense of relief! Somehow I knew that our lives would be unfolding together from here on and that we merely needed to be receptive to this unfoldment.

Later in the course of developing our relationship I would ask Lester, "Where were you and why did you not appear sooner in my life, I had been searching the Universe for you?" He would then respond, "If I had met you any sooner I would not have known how to make you happy." He too had many things to work out in his life *on the way to finding me, his Soulmate.*

There is a calmness, a stillness, a serenity that underlies the vibration of our union. Even in the midst of more coarse outer vibrations from the world around us this unifying stillness prevails. I knew that the vibration in him was the same as that in me. As we would embrace Lester would describe the energy between us by saying, "Oh, it is like butter, it is so smooth."

We began the work of building a relationship. We became engaged in July 1988, and married on December 10, 1989.

Lester says of our Soulmate union, "I deserve good things. You are a gift that God has given me. I have grown in all ways with you and you help me keep my morality and to grow spiritually."

STEP 52

Responding To The Call—
My Soulmate Speaks
By Lester Nelson

My spiritual teaching had taught me to divorce my-self from many of the things of this world. By extricating myself from some of the so-called pleasures of this world I was focusing on building a new world.

I knew I wanted a loving relationship that would reflect and contribute to creating this new world, but I felt that the odds of my finding a woman that would make me happy were very slim. I was looking for a woman who understood the need for spirituality in this world in order to create the new world. I was looking for a sign, a sign that would show me that this woman was what I needed, and not just what I wanted. I needed someone who could understand me and who I could understand in return.

When I first met Terri it was just the beginning of something that I wanted to last forever. The conversations we had were enlightening, and it told me that there was a tremendous depth that we could share and explore together. She touched my Inner Self, a Self that I had been exploring. No other woman had touched me in this way. I knew this easy connection between us meant that Terri and I had to see each other again. Right away I was ready to deepen my involvement with her. I feel our connection is a deeply spiritual one. It is a connection that Allah has united in us.

My connection with other women was often a physical plane connection and not a spiritual one. Like my Soulmate describes of her first marriage, I had a similar experience in my first marriage, also a seventeen year relationship which produced three children. My first wife and I connected physically, but not emotionally, mentally, or spiritually.

During the eight years of dating that followed my separation, I would look for something to develop between myself and the women I was dating, but nothing ever did. These connections became more of a habit than a relationship. These women did not touch my Inner Self because they did not know how to. As long as I was being satisfied sexually I began to not even look for anything further in that person. It contributed to my compartmentalizing myself.

As far as I was concerned, I could not make whatever partner I had at that time even understand that I had these other needs. At times I even submerged these other needs, living for the moment, instead of considering my whole Self, my whole Being.

Being with my Soulmate has caused me to transform my attitude about male/female relationships. Earlier in my life I saw power in a relationship as dominated by the male. Both male and female have a role, but I felt that normally the male shapes and even controls the world view embraced in the relationship. So in looking for a mate normally I was looking for someone who could fit into my world.

I have learned that these thoughts can break a relationship and in order to have harmony you have to share in a larger sense of purpose, Soul purpose. I really thought that a woman's world was different than a man's world. I did not know that it was possible to connect, meet each others needs so completely, and work together purposefully as a contributing creative force to bring heaven to earth.

As we travel through this life many things happen. Some are good, some are bad. But I soon understood that union with my Soulmate was a tremendously wonderful and good thing that has happened to me. I want to do all in my power to treasure and preserve this union with a mate that touches my Inner Self. I feel so blessed that Allah has comforted me in this way. I know nothing happens unless it be His divine will.

When Terri and I are together there is an underlying peace, harmony and a comfort we experience. When we touch it is electrifying. There is a sense of tremendous satisfaction and fulfillment. The thought of being with my Soulmate is better than food and drink. I will work with her to make these moments last forever!

STEP 53

Living Together
Day To Day

Lester and I share a union that is filled with joy and we feel a deep sense of satisfaction in our lives together. We live a relatively quiet life raising a family which now includes the son that we have been blessed to have together.

I have not felt lonely since we met. He takes away the longing and the loneliness completely. We have a strong connection spiritually, mentally, emotionally and physically. Through the years that we have been together these connections have grown more and more. We are very deeply attuned at Soul levels and nurture and support the spiritual growth of one another.

On a Soul level we both express Ray 2 energy, Love and Wisdom. Our purpose in life is to teach and to contribute to the bringing of a greater measure of light and understanding into the world. The clinical work and seminars I do allows me to teach. Lester has had a long-term ministry of teaching the people who naturally come into his daily life space by engaging them to look at the deeper meaning and purpose of life.

We have now combined our efforts and skills by co-counseling couples together. Our work supports couples in honoring their journey together as mates appreciating the sacredness of their union and by doing the hard work of relationship building. I know that Lester and I are very compatible physically, emotionally, mentally and spiritually and we continue to explore how this connection can be understood at more subtle and profound levels of energy.

In a spirit of sitting side by side, rather than across from each other, we look out before us and together we try to figure out why any particular challenge or event has occurred on our path. We help one another work it through by giving each other insights, feedback and suggestions on what we see is being called forth in us from such a challenge. We are Spirit Guides to one another. We genuinely care about the work in the world that each of us has come to do. Like new petals in a flower we watch to see how the other is unfolding, ready to offer help in this delicate process.

Mentally we process everything under the sun. We spend quality time every day talking about everything from the daily news to the profound meaning and mysteries of life. We have different educational backgrounds yet no subject is off limits for us. Lester and I seek to pierce through the veil and to understand things at their core or essence. We seek to know the unmanifest or unrevealed which underlies that which is manifest or expressed.

Emotionally we are exquisitely sensitive to one another. We are very attuned to one another and are able to pick up what is going on in each other. We comfort each other and try to understand one another's needs. More and more we communicate telepathically and intuit what the other will say before it is said. We heal one another's hurts from the impacts of daily living and the world around us. Lester and I deeply love one another and are sensitive and attentive to each others evolution and growth.

Physically we are very magnetically drawn to one another. We enjoy physically touching each other and kiss and embrace frequently during the day. Sharing physical space and our physical lives together is very comfortable and comforting. Our love making is very sensual, powerful, and truly satisfying. We touch the portal of our divinity through our physical intimacy and try to understand the deeper mysteries of the creative force within us. At night sometimes we hold hands as we sleep. We find each other's touch very soothing and healing. Especially satisfying and healing is when we give each other a massage. All he has to do is touch me and I feel tremendous energy flow from him to me that is very healing, soothing, and balancing.

Maintaining a Soulmate relationship, like any relationship, requires a lot of work and commitment on the part of both partners. Like a lawn, in order to keep it rich, fertile, green and vital, continued effort is required.

We spend a lot of time talking and we communicate very well. We do have to work out communication difficulties as they arise but we are very committed to doing so. *We start with a basic trust in one another's intentions, a belief that we each have the other's best interest at heart and that we are here to promote the expansion of one another's Soul Light.*

Lester and I have dedicated ourselves to continuing to evolve the skills we need to communicate physically, emotionally, mentally and spiritually and to help other couples to know greater connection in their unions. We try to understand the dynamics and the mechanics of communication so that we may aid the couples we work with.

Lester and I seek to stay in our *mastership* as we interact with each other. Even if one of us has stepped out our mastership we vow that the other should try to stay in his or hers thereby helping to raise the vibration of the other who is acting out of their *human self* in the moment instead of their *God Self.* We do not always succeed but we succeed most of the time. We know that we are a son and daughter of God, and that the Christ or the Master consciousness dwells within us and awaits full expression.

At times my Soulmate and I hold each other and await the next spiritual step to be revealed to us. At times we arrive at a place in our relationship wherein we do not want to respond out of our own pasts nor out of our present repertoire of responses. Furthermore, we do not want to replicate patterns of relationships we see around us or that we grew up with. We do not see the union we seek to create in our immediate life space. Often we feel saddened and distressed by the amount of disharmony we do see in the male/female relationships around us and in the media.

The question becomes, Where might we turn? What might we attune to? At these times we attune to Spirit and await guidance on how we should proceed. With Lester on his prayer rug and me in my meditation corner we learn the steps of building a relationship for the new world.

As we go along, the next steps in creating a blissful union on earth are being revealed to us. We are determined to build anew. We want to build a relationship that will be a part of the New Age. We open ourselves to be in receipt of the divine ideas that come through to the awaiting, expectant and attentive mind. We know these will guide humanity in restoring harmony in male and female relationships.

We give praise often that God has seen fit to bring us together and we know that our union is a blessing. We know that much has been given to us and that much is also expected. We open to and accept the spiritual responsibility that awaits us. We don't know what God is preparing us for. What we do know is that we feel fulfillment in our lives together and a tremendous relief that our energy is not expended in relationships or in pursuit of relationships that prove unfulfilling. We await the opportunity to use our energy in the furtherance of the Divine Plan.

Our Soulmate union gives us a glimpse of divine union with God. Together, our earthly plane connection strums our remembrance of our paradisiacal state of unity with God more and more. Our earthly interactions provide successive rehearsals to a state of unity consciousness within ourselves. Together we approximate more and more our full dawning of this consciousness by remembering more and more our union with God. Our earthly union allows us to experience more a return to the source. Between us we feel a divine union of spiritual energies, before these energies precipitated onto the physical plane to express themselves as an individualized man and as an individualized woman. *As our two sparks are united we remember more the flame from which we and all creation arose.*

Union occurs within ourselves. It is a state of bliss. Through this blissful, divine, union within ourselves we experience union with our one true Self, our God Self. In a Soulmate relationship we may more fully glimpse the Unity or God consciousness that each of us is developing. Today, many are striving to find a mate that reflects this union that is within ourselves.

Elizabeth Hatch writes, "Throughout ages and ages of time, our fate brings us together again and again until we make each other conscious within ourselves and experience each other completely in body as well as in soul. Only in this divine identity can we really be the total consciousness of the whole-of the higher self! How do you expect to get the experience you absolutely need, without me?" [21]

Lester and I have made a commitment to promote one another's spiritual unfolding, even if it means letting one another go. We do not try to bind one another and yet we remain ever so close. We pray that our union will last forever, but we also say, "Thy Will be done," if it is in accord with divine will that we part.

Indelibly etched in our consciousness is that which we have been able to unfold in each other. He and I ever reflect upon how much our union has enhanced our lives. Our work on earth together has been very sacred to both of us.

NOTES

NOTES

Chapter Twelve

CLOSING

STEP 54

Defining And Going Through Your Process On The Way To Finding Your Soulmate

---

Manifesting your Soulmate on the physical plane is a process. It is a conception and you must do the work of conceiving. Surely one would not expect to have a baby if they had not done the work of sexual intercourse, or the bringing of the male and female life force together. However, once fertilization has taken place then the process unfolds naturally on its own.

There is no more to do other than just continuing in your work in the world, guarding your well being so that nothing interrupts the process until birth or manifestation takes place. Similarly you must do the work of impregnating the ethers with your heart's desire. Then continue in your service.

On the way to finding your Soulmate there is a process you will undergo. All of the Steps, Meditations, Affirmations, Prayers and Exercises outlined in this book are important. This is a process and there is a simultaneity or all at once-ness in going through the process. In other words, if you devote all your time to one or two of these steps at the underservice and expense of the others, you may not achieve the desired result.

For example, I found myself in constant prayer and invocation for my Soulmate at the same time I worked on self forgiveness, self esteem, managing strong feelings, continuing in my service in the world, and so on. If I had desired my Soulmate strongly but did not work through my self doubt or fears, I could not have received this gift of faith. I would not have felt that I deserved my Soulmate and I would have done things to reject the event of his coming into my life.

Although there are natural laws in bringing any event into manifestation, the process I underwent in no way suggests that this is the only process or that these were the only steps or stages in bringing this event into manifestation. What has been shared in these pages is my process. Your actual process may be very similar or very different from mine.

What is important to recognize is that you will go through a process. Even if you go through your process and your Soulmate does not manifest in this lifetime, remember that you will meet him or her in this Divine encounter at the Divinely appointed time. Define your own process and listen to Spirit, your own inner wisdom for guidance.

EXERCISE

Determine To Go Through
Your Own Process

Determine to go through your process
On The Way To Finding Your Soulmate
and may success be yours
in being with the one you love
in a blissful Soulmate Union.

With so many unhappy male and female relationships on the planet today and the growing intensification in the search to find one's Soulmate one can see that a Soulmate relationship has much to teach us? At this point in our planetary evolution one may scarcely find it necessary to even ask, What is beyond a Soulmate union? Yet I sense a growing realization that the love and depth of connection shared in a Soulmate union is but a rehearsal in learning how to love. By loving so fully with our entire being within the bonds of a Soulmate relationship we can begin to grow past all bonds - thus learning how to love more universally and unconditionally and thereby deepening our union with all beings.

Life has taught me that we can grow past whatever place in consciousness we now stand. We can then come to stand in a greater expanse which not only contains new revelations but revelations which dwarf our previous beliefs about the world. I am changing and evolving everyday. What I know, and feel and believe today may be different tomorrow. Even as I looked back over my journals I could see how I had changed, how I had evolved. I do not know what the future holds. All I know is that I remain ever open to the spiritual unfoldment that awaits me in this great cosmic dance.

The journey is from God to God. Your Soulmate is a wonderful cosmic blessing on your path, as you make your way toward God. Lester and I both hope this book will be an inspiration to those who have thought much about Soulmate unions, those who have not thought much at all about such unions, and everyone in between.

NOTES

NOTES

APPENDIX 1

The Seven Ray qualities of energy are described by Dr. Michael Robbins in *Tapestry of the Gods, Volumes I and II.* A comprehensive study of the Seven Rays may be found in the writings of Alice A. Bailey. An abbreviated listing follows:

Ray 1 — Power and Will

Strengths: Strength of will, strong sense of purpose, power to lead, power to direct, power to govern, fearlessness, independence, power to liberate, courage.

Weaknesses: Arrogance, power-hungriness, domination, anger, violence, unrelenting ambition, control, suppression, impatience, willfulness, destructiveness.

Ray 2 — Love/Wisdom

Strengths: Loving wisdom, power to understand and heal through love, empathy, sympathy, and compassion, inclusiveness, exquisite sensitivity, power to teach and illumine.

Weaknesses: Fearfulness, self-pity, oversensitivity and vulnerability, tendency towards an inferiority complex, over-inclusiveness, nonassertiveness.

Ray 3 — Active Intelligence

Strengths: Wide views on all abstract questions, rigorous analysis and reasoning, great mental fertility and creativity, ability to plan and strategize, ability to understand economy and handle money, executive and business aptitude.

Weaknesses: Intellectual pride, deviousness, perplexity and confusion, excessive thinking without practical action, manipulativeness, calculatedness, disorder and chaos, wasted motion, hyperactivity, restlessness, and tendency to "spread too thin."

Ray 4 — Harmony Through Conflict

Strengths: Facility for bringing harmony out of conflict, facility to compromise, mediate and bridge, love of beauty and capacity to create or express it, strong imagination and intuition, ability to amuse and entertain, fighting spirit, ability to make peace.

Weaknesses: Embroiled in constant conflict and turmoil, lack of confidence, worry, excessive moodiness, overly dramatic expression, confused combativeness, indecisiveness, moral cowardice, procrastination.

Ray 5 — Concrete Knowledge and Science

Strengths: Capacity to think and act scientifically, keen and focused intellect, detached objectivity, facility for mathematical calculation, powers of analysis, mechanical ability, practical inventiveness, technical expertise, research.

Weaknesses: Over-analysis, skepticism, irreverence, lack of intuitive sensitivity, excessive objectivity, rigid and set thought patterns, narrowness and prejudice, lack of emotional responsiveness.

Ray 6 — Devotion and Abstract Idealism

Strengths: Intense devotion, unshakable faith and undimmed optimism, single-mindedness, utter loyalty, earnestness, profound humility, receptivity to spiritual guidance, unflagging persistence, power to inspire and persuade, purity, goodness.

Weaknesses: Rigid idealism, unreasoning devotion, blind faith, excess extremism, hyper-intensity, overdoing, ultra-narrow orientation, mania, selfish and jealous love, self-abasement, masochism, unnatural suppression of the instinctual nature.

Ray 7 — Order and Ceremonial Magic

Strengths: Power to create order, manifest and work upon the material plane, power to plan, organize and perfect form, keen sense of rhythm and timing, power as a magician (ability to bring form into manifestation), power to build.

Weaknesses: Rigid orderliness, excessive perfectionism, overconcern with rules, excessive conformity (or nonconformity), intolerance of anything new (or old), meaningless ritualism, superficial judgment based upon appearances.

NOTES

APPENDIX 2

I have been interested in exploring other systems of understanding energy which have their correspondence to the Seven Rays. To explore any number of more formalized systems as a way of understanding energy you may look for correspondences with systems that are familiar to you from fields such as religion, psychology, and philosophy.

For example, I have been interested in the correspondence between the Seven Rays and the Seven Principles of Kwanzaa. (For more information, see *The Seven Principles of Kwanzaa* by Dr. Maulana Karenga.) A hypothetical correspondence between the Seven Rays and the Seven Principles of Kwanzaa is as follows:

The Seven Rays	Principles of Kwanzaa
Ray 1 Power and Will	Kujichagulia — Self-Determination
Ray 2 Love & Wisdom	Umoja — Unity
Ray 3 Active Intelligence	Ujamaa — Collective Economics
Ray 4 Harmony Through Conflict	Kuumbaa — Creativity
Ray 5 Concrete Knowledge & Science	Ujimaa — Collective Work & Responsibility
Ray 6 Idealism & Devotion	Imani — Faith
Ray 7 Ceremonial Ritual & Magic	Nia — Purpose

Bibliography

Allen, James. _As A Man Thinketh_. Devorss & Co.

Bach, Richard. _The Bridge Across Forever_. Dell Publishing Co., Inc., 1984.

Haich, Elisabeth. _Initiation_. Seed Center, 1965.

Karenga, Maulana. _The African American Holiday of Kwanzaa_. University of Sankore Press, 1988.

Michael, Russ. _Finding Your Soulmate_. Millenium Publishing House, Inc., 1975.

Peck M.D, M. Scott. _The Road Less Traveled_. Simon and Schuster, 1978.

Price. Jay Randolph. _The Manifestation Process_. The Quartus Foundation For Spiritual Research, Inc.

Robbins, Ph.D., Michael D. _Tapestry of the Gods, Volume I and II_. University of The Seven Rays, 1988.

Yogananda, Paramahansa. _How You Can Talk With God_. Self Realization Fellowship, 1957.

End Notes

1. Michael, Russ. Finding Your Soulmate, p. 39

2. Ibid, p. 21. See chapter on Understanding Energy.

3. Haith, Elisabeth. Initiation, pp. 288-289.

4. See chapter on Understanding Energy and Soul Rays

5. The inner plane is the subjective plane, that which is latent and hidden. There is a potential for what is on the inner plane to manifest in ones objective reality.

6. Ibid, p. 41.

7. Ibid.

8. See Chapter 8 on Understanding Energy.

9. There are Seven Planes, but for simplicity's sake only four are mentioned here.

10. All of The Seven Rays, including the Fourth Ray are explained in more detatil in Chapter 8 on Understanding Energy.

11. Peck, Dr. Scott. The Road Less Traveled, p. 81.

12. Yogananda, Paramahansa. How You Can Talk With God, p. 30.

13. Allen, James. As A Man/Woman Thinketh, p. 31.

14. Ibid, p. 17.

15. Nelson, Ruby. The Door Of Everything.

16. Price, John Randolph. The Manifestation Process.

17. Dr. Michael Robbins, Tapestry of the Gods, Volumes I and II.

18. See Appendix for listing of Qualities of Energy

19. Ibid, p. 66.

20. Ibid.

21. Ibid, pp. 288-289.

If you would like to order copies of <u>On The Way To Finding Your Soulmate</u> and related material, or be placed on a mailing list to be informed of upcoming workshops and lectures, you may call:

1-888-831-1503

or write:

Above the Din Publishing

P.O. Box 2506
Jamaica Plain, MA 02130